BRANDON

SHUT UP AND GO!

A MILLENNIAL'S GUIDE TO

FIGURING OUT WHAT YOU WANT AND HOW TO GET IT

SHUT UP AND GO!
A Millennial's Guide to Figuring Out
What You Want and How to Get It

ISBN 978-1-61961-408-6 *Paperback*
978-1-61961-409-3 *Ebook*

SHUT UP AND GO!

Ringworm,

Once you figure out "Who" everything else comes into focus.

Brownie

TO THOSE WHO DON'T WANT TO BE DEFINED BY THEIR PAST. YOUR LIFE IS WHAT YOU MAKE OF IT. LET'S MAKE IT HAPPEN.

CONTENTS

INTRODUCTION

WHY SHUT UP AND GO?

WHAT ARE YOU MEANT TO DO? WHAT KIND OF IMPACT WERE you born to make? What makes you happy?

These are questions that everyone struggles with. I spent years asking myself these questions and going in circles trying to find the answers. I worked hard and tried to live right, but I wasn't living the life I really wanted. I wasn't even sure of my goals.

Maybe you're in your first job out of college and finding out it's not what you really wanted to do. Maybe you're thirty and have had several jobs, but you don't feel you're really getting anywhere. Or maybe you're a little older and still trying to figure out what your passion is and how to live it every day.

Wherever you are in life, I'm glad you've found your way to this book. *Shut Up and Go!* is a handbook for life and work. It is a handy user's guide to getting where you really want to be.

It's a method I developed after much trial and error, as I gradually learned life lessons at home, at work, and after much thinking, reading, and, most of all, doing.

HERE'S HOW

I'm an entrepreneur from a broken home who went from having to work my way through high school and college to building the life I really wanted.

I've had my share of doubts and hard times, but I've reached the point where I can say that my life is 100 percent mine. Every day I do what I want. I live the experiences I want to live, and I have the kind of life I want to have. I can afford to buy the things that I really want, and I have healthy relationships with people who care about me as much as I care about them.

I know you want the same. I also know that if I have it in me, you have it in you also. We're not so different. You've had your own hard times, and you have your own abilities. You just have to know how to use them.

I started and left several businesses before finding my way to one that really worked for me. It seemed I was always frustrated in what I was doing, yet I was still determined to get somewhere. I wanted something more out of life, something more than just the normal routine. I didn't know exactly what it was, where it was, or how to get there. Does that sound familiar?

Along the way, I sought out many inspirational speakers who got me all fired up with ideas about "what" I should do to take charge of my life, but I always woke up the next day in the same old place. These people never told me how to change my life.

It took a while, but I found out what I wanted out of life wasn't just success in business but self-fulfillment. By trial and error, I found out how to get there.

Although I'm an entrepreneur, this book isn't exclusively about business, unless we mean the "business" of life. It wasn't until I figured out how to orient my life that I started to gain real traction. I've come to learn that we can truly have whatever we want in life if we're patient, focused, and willing to do the heavy lifting. Of course that's easy to say, but how is it done?

In *Shut Up and Go!* you'll find out. It's a method that allows you to have fun along the journey, while working toward your destination. Even if you don't yet know what your destination is, you'll find that by following my steps, opportunities will begin to open themselves to you. It isn't magic; it's a process of self-discovery. And in the following pages, I'll show you how to get there.

ASTONISH YOURSELF

Many people hesitate to start something because they're afraid to fail. Oftentimes people are so tied up from worrying about what others think or say that they can't take action. Basketball great Michael Jordan put it this way, "I can accept failure, everyone fails at something. But I can't accept not trying."

We hear other people telling us why we can't do this or that.

We listen to voices in our heads telling us why something won't work. When I launched my first start-up, people told me there was no way I could land a major company as my first client. I believed them, so I started going after small companies. As it turned out, they were wrong. The first company my partner and I landed was MasterCard Worldwide.

It's those negative voices that say, "No you can't," that we need to tune out. We need to tell them to "shut up."

So the first step in my method is to ignore the negative voices, and I'll show you how.

The next step is "go." Just the act of doing puts the universe in motion and can begin to change your life. And part of "go" is letting go. Let go of the voices and associations that limit you, because it's only by doing that we learn what works and what doesn't. It sounds simple, but of course it isn't. It's a process that I'll explain step by step.

Inventor Thomas Edison, who knew something about trial and error, said, "If we did all the things we are capable of doing, we would literally astonish ourselves."

It's time to astonish yourself.

We'll set out on this journey together. I'll show you where I came from and how I reached my destination. Chapter by chapter, step by step, my method will unfold, taking you toward your own distinct path. Then you can leave me behind, or you can keep my handbook in your back pocket or on your tablet, whatever suits you.

So let's get started. Are you ready? I hope you are, because it's time to make some changes. It's time to shut up and go!

WHO THE HELL IS BRANDON DEMPSEY?

WHEN I WAS IN HIGH SCHOOL, I HAD A CLOSE FRIEND WHOSE parents lived life doing what they wanted on their own terms. Money wasn't a factor and time didn't impede them. They would take vacations as a family every year and their whole outlook on life centered around quality experiences and time together. Things weren't that way in my home. My parents divorced when my sisters and I were young, and we struggled in a single mother-led household with barely enough to get by.

The Division of Family Services visited our home many times after receiving complaints. When I got a little older, the violence and negativity turned worse and culminated in some pretty bad incidents. I carried a lot of pain and anger.

In my early teens, I lived with my mom, but we never got along. I desperately wanted a better life, a different life, and I found it outside the home, at work. At twelve I started cutting neighbors' lawns and hired other neighborhood kids to help me do it. Two years later, I got my work permit and applied for a job at a nearby McDonald's. I'd ride my bike to work and put in as many hours as I legally could. I enjoyed working there; it was a team atmosphere, and I learned a lot about keeping a smile on my face no matter how angry people got over pickles on their burgers when they'd asked for none.

My stepmom heard that the gymnastics club where my sister trained was looking for male coaches, and she encouraged me to apply. Honestly, I wasn't really interested at first, but when I heard I'd be the only guy among all the high school girl coaches, I was all in. I loved coaching. It started me on a path to certification as an NCAA gymnastics judge. Coaching eventually helped me work my way through college, and during my first years after college, I sold gymnastics equipment across the United States.

GOING MY OWN WAY

Work was my outlet, but home was a constant battle. So at sixteen, I moved out of my mom's home and went to live with my dad. My mom insisted that I was ruining my life, and my grandfather told me he'd disown me and write me out of his will. Nonetheless, I stood my ground. Life wasn't easy those first few years living with my dad. Both he and my stepmom lost their jobs and weren't able to pay my high school tuition. I loved where I went to school, and leaving wasn't an option for me. To make ends meet, I scrubbed toilets and took out the trash at my high school. They called it "grant in aid." It wasn't fun, but I did have a newfound freedom to explore, to learn, and to be myself. That was when I realized it was up to me to create the life I wanted.

In college, I started out as an English major but graduated with a bachelor's degree in communications. I didn't have a clue about what to do for a living. I met my wife, Adriene, who came from a background much different than mine. She'd grown up in a household where she never wanted for anything and was very sure of herself. She knew what she wanted out of life and work and had a certain inner contentment that I just never had.

I worked long weeks after college selling gymnastics equipment, and although I enjoyed it and the money was decent, something was nagging at me. I wanted to accomplish more, but I didn't know what. Something inside kept telling me I was capable of more: making more money, having more influence, becoming more successful. I just couldn't figure out a path forward. The fact was I didn't know what made me happy.

I was always brainstorming business ideas and telling my father about them. During one conversation, we were talking about the new construction for a major highway in St. Louis, one of the largest projects the city had ever tackled. Construction was expected to have drastic effects on commuters and the city's financial district. For me, the impending disruption was the beginning of an idea.

I decided to try to launch a company that would help businesses set up work-from-home programs. My dad introduced me to one of his coworkers who worked in human resources at a large telecommunications company, and she and I formed a company aptly named SuiteCommute.

We spent an entire summer building a business plan. We began marketing our services to small businesses, and by October, we'd landed our first client. To our surprise, it was MasterCard Worldwide, which, as I've already said, was my first core lesson in the "business" of life: don't believe the naysayers who tell you to aim low.

The future seemed amazingly bright. We had our first major customer, a six-figure contract, and I was just twenty-two years old. I remember thinking, "This is going to be a piece of cake. If I can just get one of these clients a month, I'll be a millionaire before I'm twenty-five. Then I can figure out what I really want to do."

PAYING THE TOLL

The next few years proved that it's much harder to build a company than I thought. We didn't really know how to make SuiteCommute a thriving business. We didn't have the experience, the network, or adequate funds to invest in growing the company. I was still coaching gymnastics to make ends meet. I wanted to focus on SuiteCommute full time, but we just couldn't find enough clients to make regular revenue. I felt so lost and confused that I started going to church two days a week, praying to God to help me figure out what my path was.

We kept at it, eventually landing some good customers in North Carolina and New York. Just as we were getting traction and making some money, an old friend of my business partner's approached us and offered to buy SuiteCommute if we came to work for him near Chicago. After a lot of back and forth, we decided it was worth it and took the money. I still wonder what would have happened had we not sold, but it was so amazing to have someone write me a check for my company and offer me a steady job.

As part of the sale, I had to invest most of the cash I received back into the new company. That proved to be a mistake, because I wasn't happy in Chicago. Something was still nagging at me, but I didn't know what. I just wasn't content. I had a distinct feeling that there was something better for me out there. So ten months later, I decided to leave. I was walking away from something I'd built, but the "pursuit of happiness" can have a high price. I just had to pay the toll.

GOBRANDGO!

By the time I left, I'd started building websites with my wife as a side business. I would find small business owners who wanted to manage a website on their own and build them a WordPress site for $750. It was a lot of fun. I'd build a site in five to seven hours and then spend about an hour training a client to manage the site. I've always believed in the principle of teaching someone to fish instead of giving them a fish, so I was excited to share my knowledge and talent with others. It was like coaching, just on a different level.

The website business was moderately successful and caught the interest of my friend Derek who owned a company called Weber Enterprises, which sold promotional products. I helped him rebrand the company to goBRANDgo! and even built goBRANDgo!'s first website. About a year later, we discussed merging our companies to grow bigger, and eventually we agreed to partner.

While goBRANDgo! wasn't a completely new company, it felt new to me. Derek and I spent many Sunday afternoons working on the big picture plan for goBRANDgo! We went back and forth about what type of company we wanted it to be, what kind of clients we wanted to work with, and what services we wanted to offer.

Initially, the promotional products, which were the "off-line" side of our business, represented the bulk of our revenue. However, the margins were lower off-line, and there seemed to be more opportunity in the digital space. We evolved to become, as we coined it, "an integrated targeted marketing company," which basically meant that we utilized online and off-line marketing tactics to achieve targeted business goals. It's the core of what our company does today, although many of our customers think of us as the "online experts." Our focus is on achieving business goals, not just making things look pretty online and off-line.

When I joined goBRANDgo!, it was the first time I actually had employees who weren't fellow owners of the company. It was different feeling responsible for people's paychecks and rent. I had a new sense of purpose, like a mission. And that old nagging feeling of wanting to do something more, or to be something more, seemed to be going away.

Early on, we sold every marketing tool we could. If you were willing to pay us for anything having to do with marketing, we were willing to do it for you. It wasn't until a few years in that we figured out how to create more consistency in our company. We put together yearly plans for how we were going to grow. Gradually we developed a unique vision for goBRANDgo! We adopted a mission statement, a vision statement, and core values to set our course.

At the same time, on a personal level, I was beginning to feel something I'd never quite felt before. Despite my doubts, it seemed I was getting closer to a place I'd always wanted to be. I wasn't quite sure, but I knew the feeling was real.

NOT ACCEPTING LIMITS

If I hadn't followed my instincts and taken chances, I don't know where I'd be today; maybe I'd be back at McDonald's. All along I'd wanted something more out of work and life, more than what my parents had and more than what the circumstances of my life had dished out.

Gradually I found out that what I wanted out of life and work was fulfillment, and in my own awkward way, I'd been reaching for it all along. At each step along the way, I wasn't willing to accept limitations. Neither should you.

The motivational speaker and author Zig Ziglar used to tell a story about not accepting limits. He would say that if you put fleas into a cup they would try to jump out. But if you put a lid on that cup, after a while the fleas will only jump high enough to not hit the lid. Once you removed the lid, the fleas would never jump higher than where that lid used to be. They'd learned that they can jump only so high.

I see people like this every day. They tell me they can't get their companies going in the right direction because of the market or a competitor. They say they can't get anywhere in their careers because of a boss or a supervisor. Or they can't have good marriages for one reason or another. We need to ask ourselves what limits we are imposing on our lives.

We aren't fleas. We have the ability to look beyond the rim of the cup; we have the ability to jump higher, but it all starts with trying and doing. If we continue to jump only so far, to accomplish only so much, to strive only to a given point and no farther, we won't reach our full potential.

The truth is, if you try to go farther and do more, even if you find it uncomfortable, you'll eventually find a better way. With every step you take, your path gets a little easier to navigate. Some paths turn out to be dead ends and some have many more paths that split off in different directions, but it's the forward motion that counts. It's those small steps forward in learning and accomplishing, finding out what works and what doesn't that make the difference.

We all need to start jumping higher than the lid of the cup.

As another author, Jim Collins, wrote in his book, *Great by Choice*, "We are not imprisoned by our circumstances. We are not imprisoned by the luck we get or the inherent unfairness of life. We are not imprisoned by crushing setbacks, self-inflicted mistakes or our past success. We are not imprisoned by the times in which we live, by the number of hours in a day or even the number of hours we're granted in our very short lives. In the end, we can control only a tiny sliver of what happens to us. But even so, we are free to choose, free to become great by choice."

It's your choice not to accept limits. It's a choice I made even before I knew I was making it. As it turned out, it was the only way forward to the kind of life I really wanted.

WHICH COMES FIRST, THOUGHT OR ACTION?

My father and I used to have a friendly philosophical disagreement over what really starts change: thought or action.

Let's say that you want to lose ten pounds. After you've reached the point where you've lost the weight, what would you say was the first thing that put you on that path? Was it the thought that you wanted to lose weight, or was it the first walk you did in the morning, or was it the donut you didn't eat?

I always argued that the origin is the first physical act, but my dad argued that it started with the thought.

I remember those conversations like they happened yesterday. My dad and I would go round and round as I argued, "Yes, but nothing ever starts until you actually do something."

My dad would say, "Yes, but you decide what to do in your head first and that is the thought. Therefore, you must have the thought first."

We've continued the argument to this day, but I've finally determined that we're both right. Only I'm "righter": people think about doing things all the time. They think about how their lives could be different. They think about what life would be like if only XYZ happened. However, when you start physically doing things that put into motion a series of events that move you closer to realizing your goal in the real world and not just in your head, that's when things really begin to happen.

Are you willing to take that action? That's where this book is going. So let's shut up and go!

TIME TO BE SELFISH

AS WE WERE GROWING UP, MANY OF US WERE TAUGHT TO PUT others first and ourselves last. I was raised Catholic, and my mother always used the term "Catholic guilt." In our home, it meant don't ever be selfish or God might send a lightning bolt down to zap you.

As I got older, I learned that everybody was raised with some sort of guilt. A good friend of mine constantly refers to "Jewish guilt," and every time he says it, I just have to smile. Guilt over being selfish is a big part of how so many millennials were raised. But there's another way to look at things.

CAN BEING SELFISH BE GOOD?

A typical dictionary definition of selfish is "lacking consideration for others; concerned chiefly with one's own personal profit or pleasure."

But I want you to consider something: Have you ever volunteered to help others, individuals or an organization, a charity or cause? Many of us have. And how did volunteering make you feel? For most people it feels good. By serving others, you get a positive feeling. So is doing good really selfish because it makes us feel good? And if it is selfish, is that so bad? Here's a news flash: sometimes being selfish can be a good thing.

Experience tells us that selfishness can be a positive force in the world. Sometimes we may even have to put ourselves first in order to serve a greater good.

A single-minded focus on what we want to achieve may seem selfish, but it's necessary if we want to make a contribution to ourselves and society and to the people we love.

When we set our goals, we may have to be selfish with our time, with our energy, and with our focus. When we selfishly do what we enjoy, it fills us with energy and passion. This is the kind of selfishness that gets positive results. It's a way of being selfish that allows us to serve others and ourselves at the same time.

It's a fact of life that finding your own way requires this kind of selfishness. We need to pursue and enjoy what we do in order to get anywhere worthwhile. If we give our thoughts, energy, and free time to something that doesn't give us energy back, it becomes a drain.

DON'T FILL YOUR SUCK BUCKET

I was once taught an exercise that I'd like to share with you.

It demonstrates what gives you energy and what drains you. Until I tried this exercise, I was not fully aware of how draining it was to spend most of my time doing things I didn't enjoy.

Here's what you do: grab a blank sheet of paper and draw a line vertically down the center and another line horizontally across the middle of the page to make four equal sections.

At the top of the upper-left section, write the heading, "Love to Do and Would Do for Free if Money Was No Object."

In the upper right-hand section, write the heading, "Like to Do and Am Good At."

In the lower-left section write, "Can Do, but Don't Enjoy."

Finally, in the lower-right section, write the heading, "Hate Doing and Suck At."

Now, think about all the things you do in a week. They can be personal or work related, including everything from cutting the grass and sending e-mail, to leading meetings or closing new business. Just think about the things you do and list them in the section that best describes your feelings about the activity.

In the "Love to Do and Would Do for Free if Money Was No Object" section, be sure to get as specific as possible. These are the things that give you the most energy in life and leave you the most fulfilled. Some may easily transfer to making money and others aren't money related at all, such as a hobby or exercise. The activities in this section are the ones that give you energy and a passion for life.

In the upper-right section, write down the things you "Like to Do and Am Good At." These are activities you enjoy doing and are also quite good at. You should fill this section with tasks that may correspond to your work, but not necessarily. They are activities you simply enjoy and are skilled at and that others would agree you do well.

In the lower-left section where you wrote, "Can Do, but Don't Enjoy," you will probably list many items. These are generally tasks you have to do and are pretty good at, but sometimes avoid. They are responsibilities such as chores at home or tasks at work that are part of the job. For me, the stuff that falls in this box includes things like scheduling, coordinating meetings, logistics, and e-mail. I can do those things, but I don't particularly enjoy them.

The lower-right section where you wrote, "Hate Doing and Suck At" is your "suck bucket." These are tasks that you probably procrastinate on the most and really don't like doing. You may be better than some people at accomplishing these tasks, but when you do them, your mind is generally in another place, and you are wishing you were doing anything else. My suck bucket is full of things like vacuuming the carpet at home, bookkeeping at work, setting up social media accounts for clients, or putting content on websites for clients. It's all stuff I can do, but I really hate to do. It's stuff that I generally put off until I can't put it off any longer.

Now let's look at your lists.

All the activities above the horizontal line give you energy and fill you up. All the activities below the line drain your energy.

If you're like most people, 80 percent of the things you do day to day are below the horizontal line with a large percentage of them in your suck bucket. No wonder so many people can't accomplish their goals. They spend too much of their time doing things they hate!

How would your life be different if you found ways to get rid of all that stuff in your suck bucket?

You'd have more time for doing the things you love and are great at. For instance, I used to have cutting the lawn in my suck bucket. I hated doing it. I would drag the mower out every Saturday and just sweat through the whole thing. Then I'd be tired, somewhat crabby, and just zapped for the rest of the day. When I realized this, I decided my time would be better spent working and spending time with my wife, Adriene. I found a company to cut our grass for twenty-five dollars, which was less than what I made in an hour of work. Since I stopped cutting grass, I have filled those hours with much more productive things that make me money and fill my energy bucket.

Successful people figure this out and build their success on the things they're great at. The more things you can get out of your suck bucket and off your plate, the more time you'll have to do the things you excel at. And the more time you spend doing those things, the more time you'll have to progress toward your goal and get what you want out of life. You'll find that you can automate most of the stuff in your suck bucket or hand them off to someone else.

If you really want to take the exercise to the next level, place your lists on your desk, and as you go through the week, keep track of all the tasks you do and list them in the appropriate sections. You'll be amazed at the number of small tasks that wind up below the line.

By the end of the week, your lists will probably be pretty messy and full. Now notice which lists are the longest. How full is your "love-to-do" section compared to your suck bucket? My bet is that you'll have more things below the line than above it.

SELFISH WITH A PURPOSE

You can be selfish for the right reasons. It doesn't mean you're bad or uncaring. It's a necessary part of setting goals and achieving them. It's how we learn and fill ourselves with energy as we progress.

Achieving what you want in life needs to be a fun and rewarding experience. That doesn't mean it will be all fun. You'll still have to do some things you don't like. But I can promise that if you follow the steps in this guide, even if you don't yet know your destination, you'll begin to enjoy the journey a whole lot more.

WHAT'S IMPORTANT?

EVERYONE'S DAYS ARE FULL OF MUNDANE TASKS AND EVENTS that require attention and focus. Social media updates, text messages, e-mails—they all take time. If you're like me, you're good at multitasking. You enjoy "firefighting," thinking on your feet, working on a project while watching a movie, writing e-mails while talking on the phone.

As millennials, we have trained our brains to think quickly, react, and carry us forward to the next task that requires only part of our attention. The problem is that when our minds are in firefighting mode, we don't have adequate focus and attention for the more important things.

SEEING THE BIG PICTURE

I remember closing my next big client after MasterCard. I woke up early, dressed in my nicest suit, gathered my materials, and arrived for the meeting an hour early just to be safe.

I exited the elevator to a huge lobby on the twentieth floor of an office building in downtown St. Louis. I was nervous, excited, and utterly scared.

The meeting went well, and at the end, my prospect told me they'd like to move forward. I was elated. I shook his hand and calmly walked out of the building. When I got to the parking garage, I jumped for joy and gave multiple high-fives to the air in celebration. I called my dad from the car to share the good news, turned right out of the parking garage, and drove two blocks. As I signaled to turn left through the next intersection, I heard a horn blaring and then *boom*! I threw down my phone, pulled over, jumped out, and asked the other driver if he was OK.

He was all right; we both were. Without thinking I told him, "My light was green." That's when a bunch of cab drivers came over and told the other driver, "Your light was green. He blew right through that red light." It was 100 percent my fault. I'd been preoccupied with talking on the phone and drove right through a red light. I apologized and we exchanged insurance cards. I felt terrible and immediately swore off talking on the phone or texting while driving unless I'm using a hands-free device.

That incident got me thinking a lot about what I miss in life because I'm too busy. What stoplights am I blind to because my attention is divided? What am I missing? I realized that when my head and hands are full of so many small tasks, I miss the bigger picture.

I was busy missing the warning lights.

Once when I was traveling the country for work, having the time of my life on an expense account in New York, California, and Florida, I stayed at the Fontainebleau in Miami, a very famous and luxurious hotel where the chandeliers cost over $1 million each and the lobby becomes a nightclub every night. I was out to dinner with clients, racking up a $1,500 tab, when my phone buzzed continuously in my pocket. I hit the silent button three or four times until I finally excused myself and went off to take the call.

I picked up to the sound of my wife crying and telling me, "I'm done! If you want to keep traveling like this, I don't know how we're going to make it. The dogs are sick, there's crap all over the house, and I've been home without you for two weeks!"

I'd been spending an average of twenty-three nights a month away from home, and she'd had enough. In that moment, I realized that I had to reevaluate my priorities. What was more important to me, my marriage or my job? I tried to rationalize why she should understand the importance of what I was doing, but I knew she was right. I'd been neglecting our relationship.

Over the next few months, we worked on changing my travel schedule, and she began to join me on trips whenever possible.

I'd been missing the big picture again. Yes, financial success is important, but so are relationships, especially my marriage. I knew I had to get the whole package right.

TIME BLOCKING

What's really important? For me it's having a great marriage, financial success, being a good boss, advancing entrepreneurship in younger generations, and being a role model both as a person and in business. My goal is having self-fulfillment both personally and professionally. But when I slip into firefighting mode, I find I'm no longer able to focus on what's really important. I lose track of my major priorities, my larger aspirations in life.

In order to achieve my goals, I have to make sure I plan time for what's really important to me.

For example, I plan lunches with my staff months in advance and plan their six-month reviews by setting a recurring calendar reminder. This ensures that there's time for us to talk and opportunities for them to express feelings about their jobs and the company. They know I value their input, and I work to keep them in the loop.

If something is important, you have to plan and book it.

Each week I schedule time for meals with my wife, for reviewing my personal finances, and for workouts. I know from experience not to wait for the warning lights.

So when I first decided to compete in a full Ironman Triathlon, I knew I was going to have to step up my time-management skills. Balancing the needs and expectations of my family, employees, and clients was definitely going to be a challenge. I already worked nights and weekends, so the thought of squeezing in thirty hours of workouts seemed impossible. But

I took the challenge head-on. I researched time-management techniques, and after failing with several of them, I discovered the best tool for me: time blocking.

It's a system for booking every day solid. In time blocking, you simply schedule chunks of your calendar to work on the important things.

To prepare for the Ironman, I blocked out my weekly schedule to include:

- FIFTY HOURS FOR WORK
- THIRTY HOURS FOR PHYSICAL WORKOUTS
- MEAL TIMES WITH MY WIFE (TWO BREAKFASTS AND FIVE DINNERS)
- TIME FOR OTHER PROJECTS

HOW TO TIME BLOCK

Weekly Planning Time: Each week, I sit down for one hour on a Sunday to review my upcoming week. I check to see what meetings I have, what projects I am working on, which people I need to get in touch with, and whatever I need to reschedule or confirm. I then book the holes in my calendar with project work and phone calls. I try to book each day solid. This has drastically cut down on last-minute scheduling, delays, and errors.

Zero Inbox: E-mail is a huge challenge for which I need to dedicate time on my calendar. I need to be prepared to respond to communications and urgent questions. I have developed a system that works well for me, and I will share it with you. As I go through my inbox, I immediately respond to and delete the e-mails I can take care of quickly. If I can't respond immediately, I file the messages in one of four folders: Client Action Items, Client Review Items, Action Items, and Review Items. Then during a scheduled time, I work my way through the various folders, responding to e-mails as needed. Generally I have a small set of fifty to sixty e-mails that I work through over the weekend.

Scheduled Workouts: I book my specific workouts far in advance so that I am prepared to make schedule adjustments when conflicts arise with work. Scheduling workouts on my calendar has proven immensely more effective than just mentally planning to work them in.

Recurring Meeting Times: All meetings that happen internally are booked on weekly recurring meeting times so that future meetings can be scheduled around them. Outside organizations or groups I attend are also booked on recurring calendar time, including slots for networking meetings that come up.

Five-Week-Out Planning: My weeks have gotten to the point where my calendar is fully booked four to six weeks out. This forces me to change the way I think about future planning and meeting with people. First, it's very easy to book meetings with people that far in advance because it reduces conflicts, and time and location are usually more convenient. Second, it allows me to schedule time to prepare for the meeting and make sure the meeting is productive.

Calendar Invites for Everything: I use Google Calendar and send calendar invites for every meeting I attend. If I check and see that someone hasn't accepted the invite, I e-mail or call to confirm the meeting is still on. If I don't get a response or confirmation, I don't show. This has helped to prevent hundreds of useless hours wasted waiting for someone to show only to find out the time or location was wrong. It has also allowed me to ensure time with my wife and to make sure that we are both on the same page (priceless).

Scheduled Project Time: Scheduling time to build proposals, work on projects, and generally "get stuff done" has helped me stay ahead of the curve. Sometimes I book time late at night, but calendar booking ensures I see it and get it done in time instead of scrambling at the last minute to complete a task or project.

These time blocking techniques have allowed me to be tremendously more productive and communicative, and they have prevented countless hours of inefficiency and lost productivity.

Give it a try. Block out time for working on things that you want to happen a week or more in advance. You'll find that time blocking provides the necessary structure and focus to see the big picture. It's an essential part of the *Shut Up and Go!* method of setting priorities to reach your goals.

FOCUS ON SOLUTIONS

HAVE YOU EVER THOUGHT ABOUT BUYING A CERTAIN TYPE OF car and suddenly you see it on the road everywhere you go? Or have you ever been trying to work out a problem and you wake up in the middle of the night with the answer? Seems like magic, doesn't it? That "magic" is actually our subconscious at work in a process called "reticular activation."

I credit my business partner, Derek Weber, for a talk he gave on this subject. It turns out that a certain area of the human brain called the "reticular activating system" is responsible for controlling our subconscious focus by sensing things around us and sorting them out.

A lot of people I meet go through life thinking that life happens *to* them. They think life is a series of disconnected happenstance. The fact is, the keys to happiness and success are all around you, but you have to train your brain to actively focus on solutions and opportunities. In other words, we can train our reticular activating system to be more consciously aware.

The "trick" is telling your brain what you want it to look for.

WHAT MAKES A MESSAGE STAND OUT?

The average person sees as many as five thousand marketing messages a day, but how many actually stand out? The ones that stand out are the ones that trigger our reticular activating system because they contain something we might be interested in buying or learning more about.

Our subconscious mind lurks in the background, sensing that we might *someday* want that thing. It programs itself to look for certain signs, and when those signs present themselves, our subconscious mind shoots an instant message to our conscious mind.

This is the power of reticular activation. When you harness this instinctive power, it gives you the ability to train your subconscious mind to sort through infinite daily stimuli, filter them for opportunities, answers, and solutions and then to push those messages to your conscious mind. Then you can take action.

HOW TO HARNESS YOUR SUBCONSCIOUS

The way to harness your reticular activating system is to keep your conscious focus on solutions instead of problems. Unfortunately, most of us do the opposite. We focus on problems and our reticular activating system looks for things our subconscious sees that make that problem seem larger.

Our reticular activating system doesn't know what to focus on; it just tries to give our brain more of what it wants. If our focus is on problems, pain, and suffering, that's what our reticular activating system gives us. If our brain wants solutions, answers, and opportunities, the system looks for those things. Have you ever heard the quote, "misery loves company"? It's so true! Think about the people you have met who are always complaining about life. They have programmed their minds to look for everything in their day that makes their lives miserable. Thus they "see" only misery everywhere.

WHAT DO YOU WANT?

People always say they want answers, solutions, and success, but they aren't training their brains to give them what they want. In order for the reticular activating system to give us more of what we want, we have to want the right things.

A few years ago, I was looking for ways to further monetize the massive investment we'd made on servers and technology to host our clients' websites at goBRANDgo! After years of dealing with about a dozen hosting providers to host our clients' WordPress sites, we built our own custom hosting solution at a data center here in St. Louis. This finally allowed us the control and uptime quality we needed and our customers expected, but it cost us a ton of money. We increased our hosting prices, but we were still only breaking even each month.

TRAIN YOUR BRAIN

We kept wondering what else we could do with this investment, and then it hit us: offer our new custom hosting solution to other web developers (what some would consider competitors). As we opened up our service to them, many of those developers were worried that we were trying to steal their clients. We explained that that wasn't our intention at all. In fact, we were making their jobs easier. We didn't want their clients. Our service was created specifically for web developers to service their own clients. The service didn't light the world on fire, but a few large agencies in St. Louis took note. One even hired us to host the site of one of their Fortune 500 clients. We did really well on that deal financially, and it helped cover much of our investment.

Reticular activation helped us find a way to make more money. It happened by focusing on a solution for how to better host websites and then on how to better monetize that solution. We increased both our abilities and our profit margin.

We can train our brains by choosing where to focus our conscious mind. Focusing on possible solutions rather than problems yields answers previously not considered.

IT'S TIME TO ACTIVATE

Do you focus more on solutions or problems? Think about the areas of your life in which you want to be more successful: relationships, career, and family. Your brain is wired to give you more of what you want. So focus on finding solutions and answers. In this way, your brain will give you more of what you need to succeed. Your subconscious will see opportunities and solutions and deliver them to your conscious mind.

This is another big part of the *Shut Up and Go!* method. Practice guiding your reticular activating system in the direction of solutions and opportunities to advance you on your path.

PUTTING WHO BEFORE WHAT

WHEN I WAS HALFWAY THROUGH MY SENIOR YEAR AT UNIVERSITY of Missouri–St. Louis Honors College, I knew I wanted to own and operate my own business. The problem was I didn't know where to start or how to decide what kind of business I wanted.

But in fact, there was a bigger problem: I'd decided what I wanted to be before I decided who I wanted to be. I let being a business owner define me before I really knew who I wanted to be as a person. Essentially, I was "putting the cart before the horse."

After graduation, I launched my first company and spent several years trying to figure out how to make the company a success, thus making me a success in the process. My business partner and I focused on getting small businesses as clients rather than big ones. We tried selling our consulting services when people just wanted to buy our training. We pushed St. Louis hard when our market was really the east and west coasts. We made so many strategic blunders that it was amazing we ever got any traction at all. It wasn't until we really started to figure out who we wanted to be as a company that we started to gain the traction we needed to move forward.

WHO DO YOU WANT TO BE?

This definition of who we are can sometimes go against what we have been taught.

I remember when I was younger, everyone asked me, "What do you want to do when you grow up?" or "What do you want be when you grow up?" The question always started with what and the expected answer was some sort of job role.

People use jobs to understand you by putting you in a box of preconceived notions of that job. Thus your job defines who you are. No one ever asked me, "Who do you want to be when you grow up?" Jobs force us to focus on job roles as our key achievement in life rather than focusing on our happiness.

This, in my opinion, is the struggle of our millennial generation. We've been conditioned to be "something" instead of "someone." If we focus on becoming someone first, however, we will be better equipped to find our way to what we truly want to do and accomplish.

So let's get started figuring out who you want to be.

CORE VALUES

Get out a blank sheet of paper and write down the names of the top-five people you most admire, look up to, want to be like, or whose success you'd like to emulate. They can be anyone living or dead, people you know personally or not. Write one person's name in each corner of the paper and one person's name in the middle. Then draw circles around each name.

Next to the names, write the qualities, skills, or accomplishments you most admire in each person and want to embody in yourself. As you write, draw lines from the person's name to each of those qualities. For example, if you chose Abraham Lincoln, you might list qualities such as honest and steadfast, as well as talents such as great orator.

Now notice which descriptive words are similar across several people's names and circle those words. These are the qualities, skills, or accomplishments you value most and would probably choose to be known by in your life and career.

Then, on a new sheet of paper, write down five to eight of these descriptive words in a straight line in the upper-left corner. Add any additional words to bring the descriptive words up to ten.

These are the words that you'd want to come to people's minds when they think of or talk about you.

Finally, combine similar words into hyphenated words and then cross out any that are left over until you get your list down to five phrases or individual words. These are your core values. They will be your compass to keep you on your path to becoming who you want to be.

Do not worry if you feel that others don't yet see you in this way. You are still finding your path forward.

You may be interested in knowing my core values. Of course they're still a work in progress. I chose to write them as sentences or statements in order to make them easier for me to remember. It also makes it easier to bring your list down to five.

My Core Values:

1. OWN MY OWN HAPPINESS
2. LEARN-ADAPT-IMPROVE-REPEAT
3. CONNECT AND BE 100 PERCENT PRESENT WITH PEOPLE
4. SHUT UP AND GO! NO EXCUSES
5. BE ACTIVELY FIT AND WHOLE

As you can see, I was somewhat flexible in reducing my list to five. You can be flexible, too, as long as you understand the way your words connect.

YOUR MISSION AND VISION

NOW THAT YOU HAVE YOUR CORE VALUES DEFINED, WE NEED to work on a mission statement for your life. An organization's mission statement is one short sentence that sums up what the company is all about. For you, your mission statement is going to be the defining sentence that describes why you exist and what drives you. It describes your purpose.

WHAT IS YOUR MISSION IN LIFE?

To figure out your mission statement, I want you to write down all the things that motivate and drive you. Think about what gives you energy in life. As you write them, remember one important thing: be selfish. Think about all the things you do, think, or react to that bring you inner joy. What are the things you do that make you feel like you're on top of the world?

Here are some things from my list:

1. TEACHING PEOPLE
2. LEARNING NEW TECHNOLOGY
3. HELPING OTHERS HAVE A SELF-REVELATION ABOUT THEMSELVES
4. ADVENTURE TRAVEL
5. EXPERIENCING LIFE WITH MY WIFE, ADRIENE
6. RIDING MOTORCYCLES
7. ROCK-CLIMBING
8. EXPLORING
9. MEETING NEW PEOPLE IN DIFFERENT CULTURES AND LISTENING TO THEIR STORIES

Now follow the simple formula statement that follows and write out as many versions of the statement as you can.

"My mission in life is to be (insert word or phrase here) who (or that) (insert word or phrase here)."

For instance, on my first try, I might write something like this:

"My mission in life is to be (a driver of extreme change in others) who (are looking to realize something different)."

Go ahead and try several different versions and then slim the sentence down to its essence. After many changes, edits, and iterations, my mission statement is:

"My mission in life is to be a spark that ignites change."

My mission comes from what gives me energy. I love to see change and growth in people. What ignites my passion is when I can help someone realize that a change needs to take place. I chose the word "spark" because it's a word that evokes energy. When I'm having the time of my life, I am igniting change in others or myself. That's what lights my fire.

A solid mission statement allows you to be very selective in the opportunities and people you should pursue in life. If it/they don't align with your mission, don't follow. If it/they do, you have a choice.

WHAT IS YOUR VISION?

Now let's think about your vision in life. A vision is different than a mission. While your mission describes your purpose, your vision describes who you want to become. It is the embodiment of how you want the world to see you. A vision is oriented toward the future. It describes the outcome of your mission.

Think about the changes that could happen when you accomplish your mission in life. Those changes are your vision.

In my vision, those changes might be, "People choose to take control of their lives after working with me," or "Companies experience exponential growth after working with me." Phrases like these help me envision the results of my mission.

After thinking about possible outcomes of your mission, write down some vision statements using the following formula:

My vision in life is to (insert a verb) + (insert a noun) + (insert a verb) + (describe a situation or outcome).

For instance, "My vision in life is to (help) (people) (see) (their lives for what they could be)."

Try writing a few vision statements using the formula. Then shorten them as we did with the mission statement.

With some wordsmithing, I was able to get my vision for my life down to "My vision in life is to help people see life's possibilities."

LIVING YOUR MISSION, VISION, AND CORE VALUES

It's important to start living your mission, vision, and core values every day. Start by writing and sending messages to yourself. Send yourself an e-mail stating your MVV (mission, vision, values). Write it out in a Word doc (or Google docs if you are like me), print it out, and keep it on your desk and on your dresser. Keep a copy in your glove box and at work. Post it where you'll see it and start focusing each day on how you can live these out.

Now, here's the tough part: For the next month, reflect each day and at the end of each week on how well you've done living out your MVV. You may even want to create a weekly spreadsheet and place a check mark next to the mission, vision, and each core value you feel you were able to live out each week. Feel good about the ones you could live up to and keep trying for the ones you couldn't. From day to day, week to week, and month to month, you'll make steady improvement. Keep doing the exercise and you'll see.

If you are unable to make check marks continuously, then your MVV needs some adjustment or something in your life is not in alignment with who you are trying to become. If this is the case, don't worry because we are going to explore how to start making changes to who you are. By the end of this book, you'll know how to reach your destination.

FIGURING OUT YOUR WHAT

AS I MENTIONED IN CHAPTER 5, WE'RE ALL ASKED WHAT WE want to do when we grow up, but first we need to find out who we want to be. Now it's time to consider your *what*.

It can be scary to discuss your what. What if your parents don't agree with what you decide to do? What if it's not what you went to college for? What if you can't figure out your *what*? That's OK. I'm going to show you one technique I use with people.

Here's what you do:

Take four sheets of blank paper and get ready for some good "aha" moments. Note: You can also go to brandondempsey.com to download some helpful worksheets.

We have all grappled with the question of what to do in life.

What I have learned is that figuring out your *what* is never a final destination. It's a journey and cycle of moving forward. Getting to your *what* is a *process* of finding out what you truly want.

What's important is to take charge of the journey and live it on your own terms. Wouldn't you rather be in charge than just floating along? Figuring out your *what* and living every day completely in your journey is a hell of a lot of fun and super rewarding. When you do finally realize your *what*, it will continue to evolve, and you are going to constantly get to a better version of your *what*.

Now for that first sheet of blank paper, I want you to start listing all the activities, skills, and experiences that interest and excite you, such as:

- JOBS YOU HAVE THOUGHT WOULD BE FUN TO DO
- CAREERS OTHER PEOPLE GET PAID TO DO THAT YOU WOULD ENJOY
- TASKS THAT LOOK LIKE THEY'D BE FUN TO DO
- THINGS YOU'VE DONE AND REALLY ENJOYED
- EXPERIENCES YOU WANT TO HAVE
- SUBJECTS YOU ENJOY LEARNING ABOUT
- THINGS YOU DREAM OF DOING
- THINGS YOU WOULD DO IF MONEY WEREN'T AN ISSUE

This exercise may take some time, so don't try to rush through it.

My own list includes jobs, ideas, qualities, experiences, and all kinds of things:

- ENTREPRENEUR
- ADVENTURER
- MOTORCYCLE RIDER
- GREAT LISTENER
- PUBLIC SPEAKER
- COACH
- SUCCESSFUL
- SMART
- DOWN TO EARTH
- TECH SAVVY
- LOVES LIFE
- LIVES LIFE
- POSITIVE ENERGY
- WORLD TRAVELER
- SMART BUSINESS MIND
- AUTHOR

Now circle the items on your list that you'd want included if someone wrote a paragraph or bio about you.

Then grab another sheet of paper, and from your circled words, combine similar words and ideas into new words or combinations of words that encompass their meaning.

Next, grab another sheet of paper and write full sentences describing what you would have to accomplish either personally or professionally for the world to see you according to your new combined list. Be sure to write down sentences that include things you would actually enjoy doing.

On my third sheet I wrote:

- DO A WEEKLONG MOTORCYCLE TRIP IN A FOREIGN COUNTRY
- GO ROCK-CLIMBING IN YELLOWSTONE NATIONAL PARK
- LEARN HOW TO EDIT VIDEOS FROM MY GOPRO
- PUBLISH A BOOK IN 2015
- TRAVEL AND SPEAK TO TEN GROUPS ABOUT MY BOOK IN 2016

Write out as many sentences as you can.

Our purpose is to figure out how you want your life to look from an outside perspective. It isn't necessary for other people to see you this way, but you should see yourself in these words.

Your inner energy and drive comes from accomplishing goals and progressing. If you don't know what you want to accomplish, you can't progress. So many people just allow themselves to float through life unfulfilled. When you ask them what would fulfill them, they don't know, or they just say "money." Well, I have a news flash: money doesn't buy fulfillment. Money usually does make life easier, but it doesn't necessarily make it happier. We'll talk more about money later, but for now, we want to focus on happiness.

Time for a fresh sheet of paper or download the "Goals Planning" worksheet from brandondempsey.com. Draw three lines down the middle so that you have four evenly spaced columns. Write "This Year" in the first column, "Next Year" in the second column, "In Three Years" in the third column, and "Someday" in the fourth column.

Now copy your sentences from your third sheet to the column that corresponds to a realistic time frame for you to accomplish those statements. A goal without a time line is a dream.

So in your "Someday" column, be sure to note an approximate future time when you can realistically accomplish that goal.

Are you still with me? This list should give you a bunch of energy and make you excited at the thought of experiencing and accomplishing these things. If not, try the exercise again. Feel free to picture your life evolving toward your goals.

In our last step, I want you to write down one of your list items for each of the categories that follow. We are going to set one defining goal this year for different aspects of your life.

PERSONAL: ______________________________

PROFESSIONAL: ______________________________

COMMUNITY/GREATER GOOD: ______________________

FAMILY: ______________________________

This is your list of goals for this year. If you are ambitious, feel free to write down a few subgoals, but be sure to keep in mind that you have one defining goal for each category.

Note: If you would like, you can plug your goals into my website at brandondempsey.com/goal-tracking, and you will receive monthly reminders along with tips and tricks for achieving the goals you set.

Now that you have your defining goals, it's time to break them down into smaller goals. We often write down huge goals only to realize a year later that we haven't achieved them. So it's time to break them down into quarterly goals.

Consider what it would take to accomplish each goal and then list those steps. For instance, let's take a personal goal: In 2013, I set a goal of competing in an Ironman race. I broke my goal down into smaller goals.

1. PICK A DATE AND REGISTER

2. CREATE A WORKOUT PLAN FOR MY WORK CALENDAR (SO MY TEAMMATES AND I CAN SEE IT)

3. COMPLETE HALF IRONMAN

4. SUSTAIN TWO MONTHS OF 90 PERCENT ADHERENCE TO MY WORKOUT REGIMEN

Set a date for your defining goals and start adding dates for your subgoals. You may only have one or two subgoals, or maybe more. It doesn't matter how many. Studies have shown that by writing down our goals, we are 80 percent more likely to achieve them.

The final step is to decide what to do each week to move toward your goals. For instance, let's say you plan to take a trip. You may want to set aside $100 each week to save for that trip. Or let's say you want to lose twenty pounds. You might plan three workouts per week and limit your calories. The idea here is to take the necessary action toward achieving your goals and subgoals that get you there. This will help you to stay on track as the year progresses.

BUILDING YOUR NETWORK

What if you are in a job that doesn't allow you to achieve your professional goal? Well, now you have some work to do. I want you to list ten people you know or don't yet know who might be able to help you accomplish that goal. You'll reach out to them with an e-mail or another type of message.

Here's an example:

> *Dear (Insert name here),*
>
> *I recently completed an exercise to define my goals for this year. The instructor challenged me to reach out to people who can offer advice on how to accomplish my goals.*
>
> *Would you mind meeting with me over coffee or for thirty minutes by phone to discuss (insert your goal here)?*
>
> *Thank you very much for your time and consideration.*
>
> *Sincerely,*
>
> *(Insert your name here)*

These people may provide invaluable advice or refer you to others who can. I guarantee that you will find someone who is able to give you some solid advice and point you in the right direction toward your goal. What you'll also find is that people will start looking for opportunities to help you accomplish this goal. Sharing your goals with others is key.

When training for the Ironman, I tell practically every person

I meet about it. Each is one more person I've promised that I will do an Ironman. It makes it a lot harder not to achieve your goals when you've made so many little promises. You are creating a system of accountability, and you are creating a network that will help you accomplish your goal. As they start to see opportunities, these people will reach out to help you. This greatly increases your chances of accomplishing your goals.

If one of your goals involves figuring out a new career path, reflect back on the things you like doing and talk with other people about them. Engage them in conversation about what kinds of jobs might reflect your interests. People make money doing incredible things. It's important to talk to other people and vet your ideas.

You can't do everything alone. I promise you that if you align yourself with the right people, they will go through whatever it takes to help you accomplish your goals. People naturally want to be helpful. If you explain what you need, they can often point you to the right path or share opportunities you may not have known even existed. There's power in numbers.

ACCOUNTABILITY IS KEY

I'D BEEN THINKING ABOUT DOING AN IRONMAN FOR THREE years. In December 2012, I finally wrote it down on my goals sheet. I remember the night. I was in bed going through my goals for 2013, and I was struggling with what was going to be my defining personal goal.

I had completed a half Ironman in May 2012 (I actually "raced" with Lance Armstrong before his steroids announcement. And while he was several hundred people ahead of me at the finish line, it was a pretty big accomplishment for me). The race took place on the island of St. Croix. I thought I had arrived in paradise. I went there with my aunt, a semipro at Ironman races, who had helped me with my training. I remember standing on the beach with jitters in my stomach.

The cannon went off and we ran into the water. Almost immediately it started raining and kept up through half of my bike ride. As the rain started to slow, we reached the most well-known part of the race, "The Beast," a three-quarter-mile hill climb with an incredibly steep grade. Most people walk it, but I was determined not to get off my bike, and I made it all the way up the hill huffing and puffing. I wasn't going to quit. By the time I got to the run, I was spent. I just wanted to die.

Earlier in the race, I had made a crucial mistake by miscalculating my salt and sugar intake. Now every fifty yards I was either farting so badly it sounded like I was pooping my pants, or I was burping so loudly that it garnered applause. Other runners were seriously starting to avoid me. I was miserable and just wanted to stop. My stomach felt like it was going to shut down due to cramps. My head hurt, I sounded awful, and I was exhausted.

As I headed out for the second loop, I saw Adriene cheering for me. I perked up, smiled, and trudged on. I had told so many people about my race, that when I got home, I knew people were going to ask, "So how did the race go?" And there was no way in hell I was going to tell them that I didn't finish. The exercise of telling other people proved crucial for that race and again in my full Ironman the next year.

BECOMING AN IRONMAN, FINALLY

My 2013 Ironman race started out great. I had an awesome swim, pretty good bike ride, and was averaging under an eight-minute mile for the first ten miles of the run. I was on top of the world, till I wasn't.

A major pain struck me right above my heart, and I was convinced I was having a heart attack. I remember seeing people wheeled off the course on stretchers and others throwing in the towel because the pain was just too much to bear. My body tried everything it could between miles twelve and eighteen to try and get me to stop, and I almost did. But I kept going.

I had told every person I'd met during my ten months of training that I was going to be an Ironman, and there was no way in hell I was going back to St. Louis only to tell them I couldn't finish. When I crossed that finish line, my body was exhausted, but my mind was racing with excitement. I felt electric and that I was forever going to be able to accomplish whatever physical feat I set my mind to.

When you set a goal, tell everyone you know. The more people you tell, the more people you will be held accountable to. They will ask you how you did, how you are coming along, and it will drive you to complete your goal. I've found that just telling tons of people is often better than having a single accountability partner.

IT'S NOT BRAGGING

When I first started sharing my goals, I remember feeling like I was bragging. But an odd thing happened that I didn't expect. People started listening and remembering me. I'd share my goals when I first met them, and when I'd see them again, they would tell me how they'd just told a friend about this guy who was doing an Ironman, touring Greece by motorcycle, or backpacking around India. It was like I got to relive the high of the race. My goals and the high of accomplishing them started to take on a new life, and my personal brand really started to develop.

It is more difficult to hold ourselves accountable if we haven't communicated that accountability to others. By saying your goals out loud and openly sharing them with others, you will find that you are more emboldened to accomplish them, and you will find a continued high of sharing and discussing the accomplishment of those goals long after. It's not bragging when you share your goals with other people; it's keeping yourself accountable!

TAKING RISKS

THE LATE DAVID VISCOTT, MD, THE AUTHOR OF *RISKING*, wrote:

> *If you cannot risk, you cannot grow.*
>
> *If you cannot grow, you cannot become your best.*
>
> *If you cannot become your best, you cannot be happy.*
>
> *If you cannot be happy what else matters?*

I love this quote because it gets to the heart of taking risks and the connection of risk taking to happiness. Are you taking enough risks in life to get what you want?

Growing up, I did not have a stable home like many of my friends. My childhood had a lot of instability caused by the nasty divorce of my parents and subsequent aftershocks. As

I grew older, I became obsessed with always having enough money for a roof over my head and food to eat. I was not willing to take any risks that might jeopardize my financial standing.

When I launched my company in my senior year of college, I still held on to my job coaching gymnastics thirty to forty-five hours a week. I was trying to grow my business, but I didn't have the time to travel. I was having a hard time setting aside time to work on my new company because I worked from 3:30 p.m. until 9:00 or 10:00 every night.

I did this for about three years until my then fiancée, now my wife, got a job where she started making a little more money. We discussed taking a loan from her father to cover my portion of the living expenses while I spent all of my time working on my company. I was scared to death. I had never relied on anyone up until that moment. Not only was I considering borrowing money from my future father-in-law, but I'd also be putting an official end to my coaching career. The team of boys I coached had just taken second place in our regional meet against one of the best teams in the country. We were doing awesome. To walk away meant taking a huge risk, and I was terrified.

BURNING YOUR BOATS

I walked into my boss's office and explained that I'd decided to leave to pursue my professional career somewhere else and closed that chapter in my life. For the first three months, I kept thinking that I should just give up and go back to what I knew: gymnastics. Then it started to sink in, and I realized there was no going back. I had to figure out how to make my company work.

We went through a lot of ups and downs, but we were fortunate enough to have another company acquire us just one year after I tendered my resignation. I had taken a huge risk, and it paid off big. That's when I learned the importance of "burning the boats."

You may have heard the story of the Spanish explorer Hernán Cortés. In 1519, he landed in Veracruz to embark on his venture in Central America. When he landed, he instructed his men to "burn the boats." Cortés knew that when the going got rough, if there was an option for retreat, his men would certainly take it. This is the key to the lesson.

Retreating is easy when you keep the option available. If you remove the ability to fall back on something, you become much more emboldened to make whatever you are pursuing a success. You simply leave yourself with only one option: to succeed.

I burned my boats when I quit coaching gymnastics. I had worked eight years to get where I was in that job, and I had achieved a lot. I had a great team, I was making good money for my age, and I felt great about my life. However, I knew I was capable of so much more. I was never going to realize my true potential if I didn't leave gymnastics. I had to put everything I had into my company if I wanted it to succeed.

HITTING SINGLES AND DOUBLES

Risk taking doesn't always have to be something big like changing your career. It can involve small acts. Each day offers a fresh chance to try something new, to start over effectively. Yes, there are things you have to do like walk the dog, eat, and go to work, but each day provides new opportunities for change that can impact your life. If you try something and it doesn't work, that's fine because then you know.

Trying new things and learning what works and what doesn't is about achieving small successes. In my company and in the nonprofits I lead, I always tell my team, "Singles and doubles win a game. We don't always need to swing for the home run."

Home runs are nice, but when we swing that hard, we're more likely to miss. What I'm saying is just try to make contact with the ball. Making contact is achieving smaller goals that lead to big ones. Smaller goals are a lot more achievable than taking one big swing for the big one. Big goals are built on smaller achievements. This strategy of hitting those singles and doubles is key to taking small strides toward your goals in life.

Take a good look at your list of goals and subgoals every day. You need to visualize what you want and take the small daily risks that will get you there. Your goals will motivate you.

As entrepreneur Gary Vaynerchuck says, "Most people talk themselves out of success before they even start."

Progress is what's important. People are afraid of taking risks because they feel it could set them back or be ineffective. People fear that others will think poorly of them if they fail.

The point of risk taking is to learn what works and how to advance toward the goals you've set for yourself. When you try something and fail, you learn one way of not doing something. When you try another way and it works, you'll have something to build on.

Risking is the art of progression and moving forward. Taking necessary risks is fundamental to the *Shut Up and Go!* method.

FAILING FORWARD

At goBRANDgo!, we challenge our team to take risks daily. Our philosophy is that if you aren't failing, then you aren't pushing yourself hard enough. We have coined a term in our company called "failing forward." When you make a mistake, you just fail forward and learn from the experience. Next time, you'll try something different.

Failure doesn't take you out of the game. Failure is your teacher guiding you and navigating you forward. Those who don't take risks will never fail and will never advance and grow. Growing and achieving your goals in life requires some failure. We need to begin to see failure as positive, not negative. Failing forward is learning, and learning makes you smarter and more capable of reaching your goals.

LIFE AND MONEY

DOING THE THINGS YOU WANT IN LIFE COSTS MONEY. WORK and earning money can be seen as drudgery, but if you are living a well-oriented life, it doesn't have to be drudgery. True happiness comes from within, and if you aren't happy with what you are doing every day, then something needs to change.

Happiness for me comes from being in charge of my life and seeking the experiences I enjoy. Experiences such as Ironman, touring Greece, or riding my motorcycle across the country all cost money. So let's look at the key aspects of money: earning it, saving it, and spending it.

How do we orient all the aspects of money in order to get what we want out of life?

EARNING IT

The great motivational speaker, Zig Ziglar, said, "You can

have everything in life you want if you just help enough other people get what they want."

This statement couldn't be truer. People often focus on trying to get what they want out of a job only to realize there's something external to their control holding them back. That's where other people come in.

The path of your career involves other people. We need others to help us along. And if we don't look for ways to help others, they aren't going to help us.

If you are working in a job that you don't like, be sure to follow the exercise in Chapter 7, "Figuring Out Your What." We all need careers that bring us joy.

One way to get there is to focus on helping people at work to get what they want. Why? Because the more you focus on empowering others and delivering what they want, the more they'll look out for you. Whether you're a server at a restaurant or an entrepreneur at a successful company, by focusing on other people's needs, you'll find that your needs are reciprocally met.

A team succeeds by helping one another achieve. The problem with most teams, though, is that personal agendas are hidden and not shared. Individuals don't get the help and guidance they need.

In my company, I constantly ask my teammates, "Is there anything I can take off your plate or help you with?" My plate is always full, but I've found that by staying focused on helping others, they reciprocate by helping me. This builds trust and forges relationships. When we have solid relationships at work, we advance in our careers, take more responsibility, and learn faster. If people think you only look out for yourself, they withhold information, opportunities, and advice. You will be cut off from the help you need along the path to achieving your goals.

OWNING IT

Everyone says you have to work hard and put in your time, and only then will you be rewarded. There's some truth to that, but too many people blindly trust the traditional path at their companies or organizations. They think that someone else, a supervisor or manager, is watching out for them and will promote them in time. Don't count on it.

You have to find your own opportunities at work. Hard work has to be combined with good communication about what you want. If your boss or director doesn't know what you are after, he or she can't help you get there. If your customers don't understand how you are trying to grow, they can't help you accomplish your goals by giving you more business or guidance.

You have to seek out those around you, communicate what you are trying to accomplish, and also look for ways to help others accomplish what they want to do.

You have to own your own work path and your own development. No one else is going to do it for you.

The more vocal you are about what you want to learn, how you want to grow, and what you want to experience, the more others will offer opportunities to help you accomplish those goals. This gets right to the heart of living a well-oriented life.

By staying focused on who and what you want to become, you can clearly articulate your needs to others and stay focused on accomplishing your goals.

SAVING IT

Now let's look at how to orient, plan, and manage your money so that you always have enough to live life on your own terms. Too many of us wind up reacting to life and constantly stressing about money.

The system I'm about to show you started when I didn't make much money. However, I still took vacations, had a nice car, and lived a life that brought me joy. I didn't have much, but I made it work for me. As I developed my system, my income grew. My vacations went from going to Florida to touring Greece by motorcycle for a week with my wife.

Growing up, we were all told to save money, but I always struggled with that. I didn't understand what I was saving it for. Saving money is important, but just like everything else in life, I feel it has to have a purpose. I save lots of money, but I also spend a lot of money enjoying life.

So the first step in my system is listing the things I'm saving for:

1. OPERATING ACCOUNT (DAILY AND MONTHLY EXPENSES)

2. RETIREMENT AND FUTURE LIVING EXPENSES TO COVER ME WHEN I CAN'T OR DON'T WANT TO WORK ANYMORE

3. TRAVEL AND VACATION

4. BIG EXPENSES (CARS, BATHROOM REMODEL, ETC.)

5. TAXES (INCOME, PROPERTY TAX, ETC.)

6. RAINY-DAY FUND

Every paycheck I receive gets divided up into these six categories. When my paychecks were smaller, smaller amounts went to each expense. As I got older and started earning more, I started increasing the amounts that went to each.

Now here's the key: Figure out how much you want to go where and then set up *separate* bank accounts for each of your categories. Deposit your paycheck and any other income into your operating account. Then set weekly transfers out of the operating account into the other accounts. Set whatever amounts you can afford and that align with your goals. These transfers will now act as bills and help to keep your financial goals on track.

Living a well-oriented life requires discipline with your finances. If you want to do amazing things that cost money, you are going to have to save that money so that you can spend it later.

Operating Account: This is the account that covers you each month. I budget out my year and figure out how much I'll spend on everyday expenses, such as groceries, gas, restaurants, entertainment, Spotify, and everything else. I charge these expenses on my credit card and pay off the entire credit card bill each month from my operating account. I do it this way because I earn 1 percent to 5 percent back on my credit card purchases. That gives me an extra $1,000 to $1,500 each year to spend on things I want. My money is making money for me. Please note that living this way takes a lot of restraint, and you have to be sure not to spend more on your credit card each month than you have in your operating account.

Your monthly budget should be covered by what's in this account. If you can't cover it, then you are simply spending too much. You may need to adjust your monthly spending habits or how much you put into your separate saving accounts. Yes, this means you may not be able to eat out as much, but what would you rather do, eat out or take an amazing trip? Go drinking all night three nights a week with your friends or buy a new car in a couple of years? Spending is all about trade-offs.

Personally, I'd rather skip one restaurant meal each week if that means covering my flight to somewhere in Europe. Just thirty dollars a week saved is enough for a $1,500 plane ticket, which is the average round-trip cost to Europe or South America. Heck, I flew to India and back for $1,500 on Emirates Airlines, the nicest airline in the world!

The point here is to figure out how much it costs you to live each month and then set budgets and limits to operate within. This is all about taking control of your money and your life.

I use a software program called Mint to track my spending, set budgets, and monitor my money. I highly recommend it for personal accountability. You can find it at www.mint.com.

Retirement and Future Living Expenses: Saving for retirement was always a hard one for me until I learned about compound interest. Every dollar you save weekly is worth $14,549 in forty years, assuming an average of 8 percent return when the money is invested in the stock market. If you increase that $1 to $100/week, then in forty years that amount becomes $1,454,861.00. That's not a bad chunk of change to have when you get older.

When I first started saving for retirement, I started a Roth IRA and began saving just $20 per week. With the aforementioned math, had I stayed at just $20/week, that money would someday be worth $506,326. And since it's a Roth IRA, that money comes out tax free when I turn sixty-five. Since then I've maxed out my contributions to the annual limits and will continue to do so until I can't (due to Roth IRA income limits).

Even after I max out of the Roth program, the law of compound interest will remain on my side. Taxes will just start working against me a bit. The point is that you need to start saving now while you are young and you can.

There are two ways to make money in life: 1) work for the money or 2) have your money work for the money. By setting aside money each paycheck for investments, you are putting away money to work for money.

Travel and Vacation: Traveling and taking vacations, exploring and enjoying life requires time and money. If you don't set money aside, it can set you way back and create strife in your life when you go to spend it. By setting aside money each paycheck, you can take a worry-free vacation or travel somewhere knowing that you have the funds to do so.

I plan for travel annually and figure out what types of trips I want to take the next year. I then calculate how much I'll have to save for the trip and start setting aside an appropriate amount each week. If I can't afford to set aside that much, I either reduce my trip cost or adjust the other amounts I'm saving to accommodate for the trip. Don't go into debt to travel, and don't think that you are enjoying life by putting trips and experiences on a credit card. It will eventually catch up to you and end up costing you a lot more money than you planned.

Big Expenses: Plan ahead for the big stuff you want to buy. Cars, houses, and engagement rings all fall under this expense. These are tangible things that bring us joy. I have a pickup truck, a BMW 3 Series car, and a BMW motorcycle. I love having multiple vehicles, and I have fun driving all of them. I own all of them outright and don't make any payments on them. When I bought the BMW 3 Series, though, I took a loan out on it. I paid the loan payments out of my big expenses account each month until I'd saved enough in that account to pay off the loan entirely, which I did.

Here's how I did it: I spent $28,000 on the BMW 3 Series. I put $10,000 down from my big expenses account and took out a loan for $18,000. My monthly payments were about $323.44 on a five-year loan at 3 percent. I also committed to saving

$200 each week in my big expenses account. After two years of saving that money and making my monthly car payments, the account was at $13,037.44. The remaining balance due on the car was $10,826. So I paid off the loan in full after just two years and still had $2,211.44 left to start saving for my next big purchase. Why did I pay the car off three years early? That was a personal choice. I hate debt.

Debt reduces freedom, and I'm all about freedom. For me, living without debt allows me to take greater risks in life. The more debt you have, the more you feel like you can't move and make decisions. Less debt means more options for how you want to spend your money instead of how you *have* to spend your money.

I've done this with my student loans as well, and I'm just about at the point where I'm ready to pay them off entirely. The more debt you can pay off, the more you can allocate your monthly income to the expenses you enjoy, such as travel, vacation, and other big expenses.

To be clear, I'm not saying that a big expenses account is only for saving to buy things someday. It is more like an account to use as collateral to buy big stuff. If for some reason something unexpected happens and your income falls, this account can also provide a cushion to make sure that your situation doesn't become a major stressor.

Taxes: In Missouri, I pay state and federal income tax. These taxes are pulled from each paycheck. When I was younger, I always tried to make sure I got a refund. I encourage you to do the same. This nice little bump at tax time is almost like a forced savings account that gives you a check every year. Take that money and spend it on something fun if you don't need it to cover other unexpected expenses. Spending can mean putting it in one of your accounts for future fun or spending it on something tangible you've been wanting.

In Missouri, we also have a personal property tax where we are taxed on the vehicles and property we own each year. This can be a large expense, so I set aside money each week to cover these costs. Then at the end of the year, I simply write the checks from my tax savings account, and it never interrupts my regular spending. In the past, I was caught off guard each year by these tax bills, and it was always stressful. If you have any large tax expenses that hit each year, plan for them now. Then they won't be surprises, and you'll be able to take care of them as needed.

Rainy-Day Fund: In life we all have unexpected expenses. Whether it is medical related, or your car breaks down, or something just happens where you need money. If you aren't prepared, you may end up spending money you don't have or putting it on a credit card, which will end up costing you more because of interest. That takes money away from big purchases, vacations, or other major expenses.

Set aside just a little money each week, $20 to start, just to make sure you can cover any unexpected costs that blindside you. Your rainy-day fund is there to protect you when your operating account isn't enough. As we get older and start families, unexpected costs will grow. Be prepared so that you are not taken under when that happens.

"SUMMING" IT ALL UP

Having the money to do what you want in life puts you in control. By setting aside money each week, you are choosing where to spend your money. Happiness and getting what you want is about making choices. The more proactive you can be with those choices, the more flexibility you'll have in the end.

How many people do you know stress about money? They stress because they don't plan and feel they never have enough. Many people really don't have enough. If you're in a dead-end job, you need to work on making a change. If you don't have the skills to earn the kind of money you need for the life you want, you need to go get those skills, either in school or through work experience. The point is, by making decisions about what kind of life you want to live, you can prepare for the costs that come with it. You can start allocating your resources to live the way you want.

THE REWARDS OF SACRIFICES

ALONG THE JOURNEY TO GETTING WHAT YOU WANT IN LIFE, you'll be presented with options that require sacrifices. Some sacrifices will be small, such as not getting as much sleep as you'd like, or working longer hours, or missing some social events. Other sacrifices will be bigger, such as staying in a job you don't love until you have enough money to start your own business or driving your current car until you've saved enough for a nicer one.

Sacrifices can be tough and can sometimes require making difficult choices. Generally speaking, the greater the goal, the greater the sacrifice required to achieve it.

DEALING WITH TEMPTATION

When I'm in training season for the Ironman, I sacrifice a lot.

I have to miss some prime networking functions for my business development efforts and shorten my work hours twice a week to have time for my workout sessions. For my longer workouts on Saturdays, I have to give up sleeping in, spending time with Adriene, reading, or motorcycle riding.

It's important to take pride in the sacrifices you make in order to achieve your goals. When we make sacrifices, part of us always yearns to take the easy way out: hit that snooze button in the morning, stay out late with friends, or stay up late watching a TV show. When temptation comes, remember to focus on the big picture. Be careful not to let a few slipups become habits.

Studies show that it takes about three weeks for a habit to form, so if you resist your temptation for three weeks, you'll find it much easier to resist in the future. Orient your mind on the long game and celebrate your strength in the sacrifices you make.

Each time you sacrifice to reach a goal, you increase your mental toughness. It becomes a positive reinforcement and a powerful motivator. Learning how to sacrifice is a key component of the *Shut Up and Go!* method.

EARLY TO BED, EARLY TO RISE

I can't even begin tell you how much flak I get from my wife for going to bed at 9:00 p.m. so that I can get up early the next morning for a workout. To compensate for this, I make sure to schedule breakfast time with her during the week.

Getting up early in the morning, everyone hates it. I hate it too. Get over it.

Mornings are an incredibly productive time. When I drive to the gym near my office at 6:00 a.m., there's no traffic. I save thirty minutes on my morning commute, and it becomes productive time working out. Every successful person I have ever met is an early riser. Many get up as early as 4:30 a.m. At one time that was a little extreme for me. I started as a 5:30 a.m. guy after much resistance, but after reading Hal Elrod's *Miracle Morning*, I now spring out of bed at 4:30 a.m. five days a week.

I love to sleep in, but I've found that sacrificing two hours of watching TV and working on e-mail gives me an hour of workout time and another hour to work on my business in the morning. I'm naturally inclined to be a night owl, but I've found over the years that a good night's rest can be much more productive than an all-nighter.

It's taken me eight years to get to this place, but rising early is now a habit. It's helped make me money and helped me to achieve many of my goals. I wouldn't think of giving it up.

REWARD YOURSELF

What sacrifices do you need to make? What could you give up in order to get what you want?

It's time for another quick exercise.

Grab a blank sheet of paper (or download the "Reward Yourself" worksheet at brandondempsey.com) and draw a line down the middle. In the left column, list all the things you will have to change in order to achieve your goals. Write them all down, from the food you may have to give up, to the relationships that may need to change. Next, in the right column, list all the rewards you anticipate for making these sacrifices. Try to write down one reward for each sacrifice.

For example, let's say you've decided to give up desserts on weekdays. In the rewards column, you might list buying a new pair of jeans when you drop five pounds. If your sacrifice is to keep driving your old car for another year, your reward might be getting it detailed every other month. The point is to come up with a small reward for the sacrifice you are making toward your goal. These rewards shouldn't break the piggy bank, but they should encourage you to stick to your plan.

Sticking to long-term goals is hard, so we need to reward ourselves along the way. The trick is to focus on celebrating yourself for the sacrifices you make. These rewards will help when you get stuck or find yourself struggling to stay focused on your goals.

DISTRACTIONS EVERYWHERE

OUR EVERYDAY LIVES ARE FILLED WITH DISTRACTIONS. EVERYthing clamors for our attention. Social media may be great for Mark Zuckerberg, but it's bad for you when you overdo it. We need to organize our lives around our goals and set proper boundaries. Setting limitations on our time frees us up for what's most important in our own lives.

Setting healthy boundaries requires that you identify those activities that interfere with having a purpose-driven life. Consider voice mail, for instance. I hate voice mail. I am in back-to-back meetings all day, so it's sometimes impossible for me to return phone calls before 9:00 p.m. unless I call from the road (hands free) between appointments. This created a major problem for me. My clients and teammates are usually expecting a quick response, and six to seven voice mails per day would pile up on my phone.

HOW TO SET BOUNDARIES

I had to create a boundary. So I decided to discourage people from leaving voice-mail messages. I changed the outgoing message on my cell phone to say, "Hey there, you've reached Brandon Dempsey with goBRANDgo! If this is a marketing emergency, please call the office at 314-754-8712 or text me at this number. The best way to get ahold of me is to e-mail me at bdempsey at goBRANDgo. That's B-D-E-M-P-S-E-Y at G-O-B-R-A-N-D-G-O dot C-O-M. And if you have listened to this long message and still want to leave a voice mail, please go ahead, and I will return it as soon as I am available."

Yes, I do actually spell out my entire e-mail address. This ridiculously long message has taken my average voice-mail count down from six or seven a day to six or seven a week, and it has drastically reduced the number of upset clients, employees, and family members. Creating this boundary gave me the freedom to manage people's requests in a manner that better suited my life. People now know to e-mail me first, and they'll always get a response that day.

Another boundary I created is the time that I start my workday. I no longer schedule meetings or appointments before 8:30 a.m., except on rare occasions. This allows time for my morning workout, which is a priority for me. Before I set this boundary, people would ask to meet me for breakfast at 7:30 a.m., which meant I had to be out of the house or leaving the gym by seven. It would throw off my whole morning routine. By setting this boundary, I'm able to get a good night's rest and a full workout the next morning without rushing. I'm more refreshed and much more productive during the day.

My business partner, Derek, sets similar boundaries for how he starts his day. He gets up each morning and works out early and then goes back to the house to take his daughter to daycare. He doesn't schedule meetings before 9:00 a.m.

Another boundary I set is "No Meeting Mondays." I don't schedule face-to-face meetings with clients on Mondays. Instead, I reserve Mondays for meeting with my team members and planning our week for success. I may have upward of seven internal meetings, but they are all to ensure that our team members can operate independently the rest of the week.

BOUNDARIES FOR MEAL TIME AND RELAXING

I eat three full meals every day sitting down and relaxing. I used to eat on the go, pulling over to a fast food drive-through for something that wasn't greasy and was easy to eat with one hand. It wasn't a smart way to eat or drive.

Running around all day and not taking restful meals means you aren't giving your brain the time it needs to relax and recharge. I've learned to make time for lunch with a client or friend and to have dinner every night with my wife, Adriene. In this way, I not only relax, but I "double dip" by enjoying food and interaction with others.

I hear stories all the time about how people are too busy to eat lunch. That's an ineffective way to live and work. Your mind and body need periodic breaks from everyday stress. A well-rested mind is a productive mind.

COMMUNICATING CLEAR EXPECTATIONS

Setting boundaries is a good habit, but it takes communication for the process to bear fruit. People you interact with need to know what those boundaries are. By communicating clear expectations with those around you, they'll know what to expect from you.

Adriene and I review our upcoming week on Sunday afternoons. We discuss who is going to be taking care of the dogs and other household chores, and we coordinate dinner for each night of the week. By setting clear expectations, we're able to optimize our time individually and collectively.

Most of us think we're setting clear expectations just because they're clear in our own heads, but people around us don't know our expectations unless they're clearly stated. When you take time to plan and share expectations with others, things work more efficiently for everyone.

For instance, I used to be notorious for going to meetings and talking about what could be done and then closing the meeting with no clear action items, time lines, or accountability for those involved. Now at every meeting, I make sure to state a person's name, look him or her in the eye, and communicate this recap formula: "(Name) will do (task) by (time and date) and notify (whoever needs to be notified) by (time and date) via (specific communication method, such as e-mail or our project management system)."

I do this recap with each person at the meeting. If someone doesn't have any takeaways, I say, "(Name) has no action items or expectations from this meeting." If we are seeking agreement, I make sure to state each person's name and ask them if they agree and support whatever decision we're making. This helps with public accountability and also helps to ensure that everyone is on the same page.

I work at being very clear with my clients about what results they can expect from working with me and my firm. Everyone wants to believe they'll see results immediately, but we work hard to make sure they understand that marketing is a process and takes time.

We set up tracking mechanisms and work each week to explain to clients exactly where we are and how we're doing regarding expectations from our previous meeting. It's tricky with sales, because you often want to communicate high expectations. The tough part is how to balance your desire for great results with more realistic outcomes. I never want to lose a sale or a client's trust. So by speaking honestly when it may be uncomfortable, I can prevent awkward situations later. By being clear and realistic about what they can expect from my company, I'm building good working relationships and saving a ton of headaches.

What boundaries do you need to set with those in your life?

It may seem easier to avoid setting boundaries and expectations up front, but in the long run, it's well worth it to set those boundaries early on. When people know where you stand, they're less likely to be disappointed. Good communication is fundamental to success.

WHO DO YOU KNOW?

IF YOU WANT TO ACCOMPLISH SOMETHING AND REACH YOUR goals, chances are you're going to need help, guidance, or assistance somewhere along the way. Everyone knows the old saying, "It's not what you know, it's who you know." There's a lot of truth to it, even if it's not always absolutely true.

People are the key to unlocking potential and opportunities. You need others to pay you, guide you, and introduce you around.

Who do you need to be cultivating a relationship with today to help you on your path to achievement?

When I launched my first company, I asked my father-in-law for a small loan to help cover expenses while I pursued my start-up full time. He graciously gave it to me because I'd developed a relationship with him. Relationships are everything, and the stronger your relationships, the faster you'll achieve your goals.

Most people don't think about the key relationships needed to progress their careers or personal growth. Some people are lucky and wind up meeting the right people through happenstance, while others never meet the right people, and they aren't given the same opportunities. As you look at the goals you established for your life, who are the key people or types of people you should be developing relationships with to reach those goals?

Who are the five key people who can help you develop your career? Where do they hang out? Where do they work out?

MY KEY PEOPLE

When I bought into goBRANDgo!, the key relationships I identified were with Derek, my business partner; Kim, a key influencer and governor on the board of a local sports club where I was a member; Todd, a business coach for a nonprofit I worked with; Steven, our accountant; and Mark, one of our major clients. These key relationships have been paramount to goBRANDgo!'s success and profitability. These people have introduced me to more clients, coached me through tough times, and guided me to developing a better business.

Derek and I met through a business-networking group. As the two youngest entrepreneurs in the group, we became fast friends. Developing a relationship with Derek was vital, especially after we went into business together. We became dependent on each other's individual success. Our opportunities and potential were only limited by our ability to collaborate, innovate, and follow each other's lead. Developing this relationship meant spending time with Derek and talking a lot about business and life in general. We worked hard to make sure we were on the same page, and we developed a unified vision for goBRANDgo! Our vision has been tested many times, and through some of our darkest moments, we have come out ahead because of the strength of our relationship.

Kim was on the board of the Missouri Athletic Club, a private club in St. Louis focused on athletics and business relationships. He was a key influencer in a club of twenty-five hundred members. I identified Kim as one of my key relationships because of his background in psychology and social intelligence. He taught me a lot about human behavior, communicating with others, and facilitating introductions for trusted partners. Kim helped introduce me to several clients and others who connected me with clients and advisers. My club membership and relationship with Kim were responsible more than 20 percent of goBRANDgo!'s annual revenue in just two years.

Todd was the facilitator of the St. Louis EO (Entrepreneur's Organization) Accelerator program that Derek and I participated in. He showed me how to better delegate and systematically grow our company. Todd was influential in helping us learn to step back and view our business critically as a system and not as our "little baby." From Todd I learned to construct a strict set of guidelines for how to run the company as its own entity, not just as an extension of myself. That meant I could demand more from the company and look more objectively at what needed to be fixed.

Steven is our accountant. If you own a business, you need a great accountant. A good one won't do. A great accountant can help you in ways you never thought possible. If your accountant is someone who just does your tax returns, you are missing huge opportunities for saving money and growing your business. Steven taught us how to manage our cash, set financial goals, and legally make a great living. This relationship has also developed into a referral partnership in which we refer prospects back and forth.

Lastly, there is Mark, one of our big clients. I met him through Kim at the sports club. Mark challenged us to become a better company. He set high standards for what he wanted to see and helped shape our company into its current form. He helped us develop a recurring revenue model, which was key to unlocking profitability for goBRANDgo! Mark guided and coached us to a business model that has made our company insanely profitable compared to similar companies in the marketing industry. Without his advice, demands, and investment, we would still be selling low-margin creative services.

As you can see, these five key relationships guided me, opened doors, provided capital, and demanded that I do certain things to be successful. Key relationships help you see the things you don't even know you should be looking for.

FIND YOUR PEOPLE

Look at the goals you want to accomplish and write down one person's name next to each goal.

When I did my first Ironman, I wrote down the name Mason Duchatschek. Mason had done three Ironman races before me and was a huge inspiration. When my training started to burn me out, I called on Mason to coach me through it. He told me what I needed to hear and gave me the encouragement I needed to continue. He even drove to Louisville, Kentucky, to cheer me on and support me during my race. Mason is a true friend and someone I needed by my side to help me accomplish the most physically demanding task I ever attempted.

People want to see you succeed. You just have to ask for their help. Everyone looks for ways to share their time, talent, and treasure. Some have more of one than another to give. It's your job to figure out what you need the most and who is capable of giving it to you.

People are the key to your success and to the *Shut Up and Go!* method.

SEEING YOUR FUTURE

"Vision without action is a dream. Action without vision is simply passing the time. Action with Vision is making a positive difference."

— **JOEL BARKER, AUTHOR AND FUTURIST**

VISIONING YOUR FUTURE IS THE ACT OF SEEING IN YOUR MIND what you want to happen. It is more than just *thinking* about what you want to happen. You need to see your vision as an accomplished fact, as if it has already happened. In your mind's eye, your vision is real, as if you've already reached your goal.

Here's an example:

I recently went through a Rusty Wallace Racing Experience in which participants drive NASCAR cars around a pro track. You can drive as fast as you want, and it can get a little scary.

Before you put on the fire suit, helmet, and neck brace, the instructors take you through a one-hour training course. (If you didn't buy the insurance upfront, then you sure will by the end of the instructional session because they do a great job of scaring the crap out of you!) One of their main points is to "look where you want to go." Over and over they say, "If anything goes wrong, remember to look where you want to go because if you look at the wall, you will hit the wall; if you look at a car in front of you, you will hit that car. So look where you want your car to go and you will go there."

Visioning is the same thing.

When we visualize how our lives will be when we've realized our dreams, our bodies and minds have an interesting way of helping us get there. Visualization unlocks a critical component in goal setting. It allows you to envision what needs to change in order to get you where you want to go. It helps you to feel the sensation of reaching your goal even before you get there. Visioning your goal actually releases endorphins, which are the chemicals in your brain that make you feel good. That's how real it can feel.

SEEING THE LIGHT

When I visioned the successful completion of my first Ironman race, I visualized crossing the finish line and giving people high-fives everywhere I went. I envisioned the feeling I would experience knowing what I had just accomplished. I visualized telling all the people back home that I'd done it. Visioning my success in detail helped me endure the grueling training schedule and helped me get through some dark days.

When I finally crossed the finish line, my vision sprung to life.

It has worked this way for me in business too. I remember going for a run one morning and thinking about what a failure I had become. I had launched my own business, but I'd had a lot of trouble gaining traction and getting any sustainable revenue. As I ran, I kept thinking that I should shut the company down and get a job working for someone else. I was working hard at my start-up but without any real purpose, and I wasn't sure where I was headed.

On that run, I remember looking up at these huge, eight-feet-tall and higher, century-old trees growing right next to each other. They were all gnarly and tangled and competing for sunlight. I thought to myself, "Each of these trees somehow found a way." It wasn't a clear path straight to the top. They had to grow and change to find their direction to the sun, and their survival depended on bending and adapting themselves.

I realized then that I had to be the same way. I also had to adapt and change. I had to see my way toward my own sun, my own future, and the type of company I wanted to create. That was a turning point. I started visioning myself running a successful small business. I saw myself traveling the world with the ability to work from anywhere. I saw myself driving nice cars and having the money to buy what I needed and wanted.

Even though I didn't know exactly how to get there, I began focusing intently on where I wanted to go, and gradually my path started to light up.

THE HOW OF YOUR VISION

A vision is the key that connects us from where we are to where we want to go. But if we don't know where we want to go or what we even want, how can we figure out the path we need to take?

Many of the people I meet wander through life aimlessly. When I talk to them, they say they are unhappy with their jobs, their spouses, their kids, or whatever. But when I ask them what they want, they tell me they don't know.

If we don't know what we want, how do we figure out the ways to get it?

The exercises I lay out in *Shut Up and Go!* are the *how* of bringing your vision to reality. As you learn to set goals in Chapter 2, focus your subconscious on solutions in Chapter 4, and figure out your *what* in Chapter 7, you are gradually rehearsing your vision.

The process of visioning can be so real that it motivates action in the present. As we visualize how our lives will be, our vision begins to compel us toward our goals. And as your vision becomes clearer, your mind subconsciously looks for opportunities that move you closer to your goals, closer to what you want, closer to where you want to go, and closer to the things you need to do to get there. Visioning tells your mind what things to look for.

USING YOUR VISION

Visioning is the key to mentally seeing and orienting our

lives toward our goals. Once we've picked a destination, we can chart a path. But without a destination in mind, we are just wandering.

As you follow the *Shut Up and Go!* method and your vision becomes more real to you, you can reinforce your vision by articulating it to others. The more you talk about your goals and share them with other people, the easier it is for them to help you along your path and to open doors for you.

By spending time each day visualizing what I want, I get a clearer vision of what I'm truly after. I suggest you do the same. Do the exercises in this book and follow the lessons I lay out, and visioning will gradually unfold for you, just as it has for me.

HABITS GOOD AND BAD

EVERYONE HAS HABITS. OUR MINDS ARE WIRED TO WORK habitually. In your high school or college classes, was there assigned seating? If not, did you notice that most people sat at the same desk every time, even though they could have sat anywhere? Habits create harmony in our minds. Habits allow us to focus on other things while our bodies and subconscious minds take care of the rest without us having to think consciously about it.

I have had many bad habits in my life, such as picking and tearing my fingernails, not listening when someone else is talking, or giving people tasks with too little information to complete them successfully.

The fingernails thing was something I'd do when I was nervous, and I couldn't stop, even when my cuticles became infected.

Instead of really listening to other people, I was impatiently waiting to speak my own opinion. This habit prevented me from actually hearing and comprehending what others were saying. I was so focused on my own agenda that I'd often miss critical cues that would have better informed me. I had to work on focusing on people and not letting my mind race to what I wanted to say. I can remember learning to concentrate on the words people were saying and thinking to myself, "What is one question I can ask to better understand their point?" This helped me focus on hearing them fully instead of just running over them with my own agenda.

I'd been in the habit of trying to micromanage people at work. I had to learn that people could manage their tasks better themselves if I made sure they had all the resources they needed up front. I found it's a better way to work as a team. I learned to balance the desire to tell people what to do with allowing them the independence they needed to get the job done.

Bad habits are tough to change. Think about all the people you know who smoke who've told you they've quit several times. Mark Twain said, "Giving up smoking is the easiest thing in the world. I know because I've done it thousands of times."

I believe people are free to do what they want. I also believe that if people really want to quit something badly enough, they'll find a way to do it. One method I've learned is to create new habits—good ones.

USING HABITS AS A TOOL

Good habits can allow us to get things done right almost automatically. It's like a practiced skill, whether it's swimming, bicycle riding, carpentry, shooting baskets, or playing a musical instrument. Our bodies begin to function on automatic because the skill has become a habit. At the same time, our minds are freer. Good habits can be powerful tools for getting what you want in life.

Case in point: If you have a habit of always hanging out with low achievers, then you won't be pushed to achieve more. But if you develop the habit of spending time with successful people, you'll be more motivated to achieve more yourself.

Phillippa Lally, a health psychology researcher at University College in London, published a study in the *European Journal of Social Psychology* on making health habitual. Lally's research showed it takes sixty-six days on average to form a new habit. We have to stick with something for several months before it starts to become a part of us.

Habits are a process, and every process involves both success and failure. Don't allow yourself to get down if you have some days that aren't successful. Success in life is all about the long game.

HOW I DEVELOP GOOD HABITS

To develop good habits, start by putting your goals and priorities on your daily calendar. This is positive reinforcement. You constantly see it and are reminded of your goal. I do this for my fitness goals, reading time, breakfast with my wife, and even to remind myself to work on my schedule!

Using a calendar frees you to live your day, as you're constantly reminded of your goals. And as you develop good habits, you also free your mind to think about more complex issues.

A great example of setting a good habit is how I make sure my car always has enough gas in the tank. I fill up and get my car washed every weekend. This way, I always have enough gas for the week and don't have to worry about stopping for gas somewhere on my way to a meeting. I no longer run late or meet new clients with a dirty car.

Another good habit I worked on is living a paperless life. This has allowed me more freedom and saved my butt a thousand times. I can now access just about any document I might need anywhere in the world, on any device. When I'm at the DMV and they ask for my insurance card, I'm able to pull it up on my phone. Last week, when I went in for my yearly physical, the nurse asked for my insurance card. I pulled out my phone and was able to e-mail her a copy of my card instantly.

It has taken some work to go paperless, because I do enjoy writing things down with pen and paper. However, the ability to share items from anywhere in the world far outweighs that old habit. I use several software programs, including Evernote, Google Drive, Dropbox, Scannable App, and Things. These apps and many others allow for information to be saved, searched, and easily indexed. Before I committed to going paperless, I used to have stuff all over the place, and I had trouble finding what I needed when I needed it. By creating habits that support my paperless lifestyle, I've freed myself up.

You can have healthy habits that help you work toward your

goal, or you can have unhealthy habits that lead you away from your goal.

Your habits should align with a purpose-driven life and your achievement goals.

To complete the Ironman, I had to spend fifteen to thirty hours a week working out and training. I had to develop the habit of going to bed early at a certain time every day and getting up early on schedule to squeeze in my workouts.

Think about all the habits you have and what needs to be changed.

I used to have a habit of going out to eat on a pretty regular basis, but that meant I wasn't able to save as much money as I wanted. I changed this by creating a weekly draw from my bank account into a savings account for big purchases. Creating this new habit eventually allowed me to save up enough money to buy some of the nicer things I enjoy in life.

Good habits create alignment and clarity, but they take conscious planning to make happen.

In business, I used to have a habit of not keeping my clients updated on the progress of their accounts. I always assumed, "no news is good news," but quickly learned that's the exact opposite of how clients think. So I created a spreadsheet to make sure I meet clients for lunch at least once a quarter, make weekly calls, and have a monthly face-to-face meeting at their offices.

These good habits have allowed me to develop deeper relationships with my clients. They have opened doors for new revenue, and our profitability has soared under this new model of increased client engagement. It has helped goBRANDgo! progress much faster, while freeing us up to work more efficiently.

Good habits give you freedom.

Changing bad habits takes time, sacrifice, and constant visioning. But once you get your habits in alignment with your goals, you'll find that your progress speeds up exponentially. Your mind starts looking for ways to optimize your life instead of just scrambling to get the basics done. You become more empowered toward your goals.

HITTING SINGLES AND DOUBLES

PEOPLE OFTEN TELL ME THAT I'M THE MOST PRODUCTIVE person they know. People who work with me see progress on a large scale. I move the proverbial needle every day.

As I mentioned in Chapter 9, "Taking Risks," it's all about hitting singles and doubles. It's worth exploring here in more depth, because singles and doubles are what we need to win the game.

When I first started working with my business partner, Derek, I was always swinging for the fence. Everything I did, I tried to hit a home run. That meant missing or striking out a lot. Every time I attempted to do something, I tried to envision what a home run would look like for that task. Then I'd try to do what I thought was needed to hit it out of the park. My focus was always on big wins and huge successes. The problem was that they came infrequently and missing a lot hindered our progress.

If you watch baseball, you've probably noticed that a batter's focus is primarily on making contact with the ball. Getting on base is the trick. That means hitting a lot of singles and doubles. What Derek and I learned is that you don't have to swing for the fence every time, just try to make contact with the ball.

SMALL WINS

The key to success is making small improvements. Small wins, as I call them. Once they start to compound, you start making larger strides. By focusing on executing smaller tasks, I've found it much easier to get things done and make progress. Each small win or hit deserves celebration, and over time, they stack up to impressive victories.

When collaborating with people, I've found that focusing on singles and doubles is much more conducive to teamwork. When I was trying to hit home runs, it was always on me to be the star. When I struck out, my team looked at me as a failure. When I hit a home run, it was all about me winning. It didn't build team loyalty or camaraderie, and it left the team yearning for a win because it was often many months between home runs.

When I switched my strategy to hitting singles and doubles, I was able to involve more of the team. We started helping each other more and progressing together. Small successes came more frequently and celebration and encouragement became routine. This energized our team and put the onus on all of us to keep winning together, every small step of the way.

The singles and doubles strategy has also helped me in my nonprofit work. I currently sit on the global board of EO Accelerator. The board consists of entrepreneurs from around the world who all share a common goal: to provide a path for entrepreneurs looking to grow their businesses aggressively. We focus on entrepreneurs whose businesses are generally under $1 million in annual revenue, and our mission is to help them get over the $1 million mark in two years or less.

Ideas come up all the time for what the Accelerator board can do to help grow the program and better serve our entrepreneurs. However, we are all volunteers running our own businesses, and many times the ideas are so huge that it would take someone focusing full time to execute them. When I started talking about singles and doubles to this group, there was some initial confusion because our overarching goal is to hit home runs. As we discussed it more, we started setting smaller goals and making the tasks easier to complete. This allowed us to build momentum and group consensus.

For example, one of the ideas we discussed early on was the need for a shared communication portal. We discussed how it would single-handedly get everyone on the same page and standardize how to run the dozens of different programs worldwide. However, building and launching a portal that included calendars, document sharing, member tracking, and every other aspect of a nonprofit group was a pretty daunting task. So we broke it down into steps.

We found communication software that already existed and set small goals to accomplish each quarter. Instead of the goal being to have a completed portal fully up and operational with all the modules and components, we set a goal of first having two components up and working. We hit our goal, invited all members to access the site, and it was a huge success. Then we started setting goals for releasing new modules every six months. We were building on singles and doubles. As we gained momentum and traction, other opportunities started opening for the board to attract more people and more support for EO Accelerator. Singles and doubles were key to our success.

As you think about your goals, consider the small wins you'll need to get there. If you're always expecting to hit home runs, you'll find it's more difficult to know where to start. This is where most people I speak with get hung up. They put all of their energy into getting one big thing to happen. They want to hit that home run. Instead, try looking at your goal from different angles and breaking it down.

What are the small steps you can take now to make progress? By hitting singles and doubles, you will find that you're able to build steady progress, and that's what wins the game in the long run. You'll have more control and momentum, which is incredibly powerful.

FOUR STAGES OF LEARNING

ACCORDING TO NEUROLINGUISTIC TRAINERS JOSEPH O'CONNOR and John Seymour in their book, *Introducing NLP*, there are four stages to learning:

1. UNCONSCIOUS INCOMPETENCE

2. CONSCIOUS INCOMPETENCE

3. CONSCIOUS COMPETENCE

4. UNCONSCIOUS COMPETENCE

Unconscious incompetence is when we *don't know* what we don't know. When we aren't aware of something, we are *unconscious* about it.

For instance, when I first started my business, I didn't know that cash flow was more important than profitability in a small business. I knew nothing about cash flow; I didn't know it existed. I was completely unconscious of it. I also didn't know how to use it. I was *incompetent* at it.

Conscious incompetence is when you *know* what you don't know. For instance, I know I can't fly a plane; therefore, I am *conscious* of my *incompetence* (I know that I don't know how).

I can decide if it's something I want to learn. This stage of learning is vitally important, because we all are consciously incompetent about many things. Do we want to learn more about them or not? Do we want to remain incompetent or do we decide that in order to get what we want we have to become competent at something new?

Your choices are to learn what it takes, to give up the goal, or to hire someone else to do it.

Let's take the plane example again. If my goal is to vacation in San Diego, I can either learn what it takes to fly a plane, hire an airline to fly me there, or not go at all.

We make these decisions every day.

Conscious competence is the awareness of knowing how to do something. To become consciously competent, you have to learn how to do something. You have to seek out resources, such as people, books, or information online. The more you learn, the more consciously competent you become.

When I first started traveling, I would tell people all about my adventures. Then I got the idea to make some videos of my travels, but I had no idea how to go about it. I was consciously incompetent, knowing that a video was a great idea, but it was something I didn't know how to do. So I decided to learn.

I bought a GoPro camera and downloaded iMovie on my iPad to start making videos. I watched all sorts of YouTube videos and asked some friends to show me some moviemaking tricks. I learned that it's better to shoot shorter clips because it makes editing easier. As I learned more and more, I gained conscious competence and eventually got pretty good at making videos. But I was far from being a master moviemaker.

Unconscious competence is the ability to do things without having to think about them. Unconscious competence is mastery.

Have you ever heard sports figures talk about how their playing is just "second nature?" That's where unconsciously competent abilities come through. It took a lot of practice to develop those skills to their full potential. Things you are unconsciously competent at doing are often the things others say are your special gifts or talents.

On the everyday level, we learn to be unconsciously competent at many tasks. For example, when I brush my teeth, I'm not thinking about the act of brushing my teeth or what I need to do to get them clean. I'm simply going through the motions, and my mind can wander in many different directions. When you become unconsciously competent at something, new opportunities are revealed that you were never able to see before.

BECOMING A MASTER

Something I worked very hard to master is public speaking.

When I was a junior in high school, I took a public speaking class. When I signed up, I was unconsciously incompetent as to how vital public speaking would be to my career.

Public speaking is often ranked as the biggest fear people have, ranking even higher than death in many studies. This means that good public speakers really stand out. I knew I wanted to stand out, so I was committed to learning.

Our first assignment was to give a speech teaching the class how to do something. Everyone picked something different: how to wax your car (where a guy brought in the door from his Jeep), how to ask a girl out (I went to an all-boys school, so this was of huge interest), and how to throw the perfect football spiral (taught by our school's varsity quarterback who was unconsciously competent at that).

I thought long and hard and decided I would demonstrate how to make a potato gun. I had recently completed my first potato gun and knew the difference butane makes as a fuel source over hair spray (butane is not recommended, it is way too powerful and dangerous).

I prepared for the day with note cards reminding me to look people in the eye and talk slowly, along with other tips to keep people's attention. On the day of my presentation, my stomach was in knots. I finally gave the presentation with sweaty hands and stuttering words, but I did OK.

Years later, when I launched SuiteCommute, I tried everything to get leads—cold-calling, trade shows—but it was tough going. Then I started to do some speaking engagements, and the leads began pouring in. The problem was that I was still a nervous wreck before speaking. Over time I got better. With each presentation my words flowed more easily. My body language got stronger, and I started learning rhythm and cadence. I learned when to use humor, how to warm up a crowd, and how to keep people engaged.

Public speaking gradually became second nature for me. In time, I became unconsciously competent. Today I can talk in front of just about any size crowd, and I have a great time doing it. I'm able to focus 100 percent on my message and let my body and mind take care of the rest. It took a lot of practice, learning hand gestures, timing of jokes, solicitation from the crowd, movement around the room, and many other tricks of the craft.

What skills do you need to master? What do you need to become *unconsciously competent* at to achieve your goals? With enough learning, dedication, and perseverance, you can become a master of anything. You may even learn to fly a plane to San Diego.

GETTING YOUR PRIORITIES STRAIGHT

"Decide what you want, decide what you are willing to exchange for it. Establish your priorities and go to work."

— ***H.L. HUNT, ENTREPRENEUR AND OIL TYCOON***

ANY FORMULA FOR SUCCESS, NO MATTER HOW SIMPLE OR straightforward requires sticking to it. You have to learn how to structure your life so that you can focus on your goals.

In my twenties, I struggled to grasp this level of focus. As I entered my senior year of college, I had no clue as to what I wanted to do for a career. I knew I wanted a professional career outside of coaching gymnastics, but I didn't really see what would become my "real job."

As you read in Chapter 1, I started SuiteCommute and sold

that company four years later, but even then I didn't know what I wanted out of life. It wasn't until I was able to crystallize what I wanted that I was able to figure out how to get there. In the exercises presented in Chapter 7, "Figuring Out Your What," you began the process of finding out exactly what you want to accomplish. Once you have figured out what you want, it's time to align your priorities.

ALIGNING OUR PRIORITIES

We have lots of priorities in life. Home, family, and work are often our major priorities. But we also need smaller priorities, particularly those focused on getting things done. Setting these priorities means choosing what you want to focus on first.

I tend to gravitate to tasks that are easy to complete. I do this all the time with e-mail. I will put off working on a larger project so that I can knock out a bunch of simple tasks in my e-mail and feel good that I got a lot done. It gives me a sort of false temporary high, but takes away time from making progress on my larger projects. And that's the rub. We need to align our smaller priorities with our larger projects in order to achieve our goals.

For instance, as a part of our process at goBRANDgo!, we build monthly reports for our clients to show what our marketing has accomplished. We pull metrics and data from Facebook, Google Analytics, tracking, and other marketing software. Once we have compiled all of this data, we have to make it legible and easy for our clients to use. This whole process takes about two hours for us and about ten minutes for the client to review and say, "OK, looks good." So I decided to find existing software to automate the building of these reports so they take less time to create. That seems pretty simple, right? I thought so too.

It was November, and I set a goal to have it figured out and built by the end of 2014. I blocked out three days to spend two hours each day to research it. Those six hours flew by. I'd investigated ten different programs but hadn't found the one I needed. I reworked my calendar and told myself I needed to make a decision in the next two-hour time block.

I chose the software and began running it for one client. The problem was that it took three hours to set that client up properly, and I had another fifteen clients to go. I was happy that I'd found a solution, but I was worried about the time it would to take to set it up for all of my clients. I had two weeks before the end of the year, which was the goal I'd set. I realized that if I wanted to remain committed to my goal, I needed to readjust my priorities over the next few weeks.

Readjusting my priorities meant moving meetings and other tasks so I could tackle this large project. Yes, it would have been easier to extend my deadline, but I've learned that extensions only lead to more procrastination. I blocked out two entire days to get it done. I knew I would be more efficient if I was working the same task for multiple clients.

I worked those two days nonstop, not even checking e-mail, and got all the clients set up. Then on January 1, 2015, I clicked a button and all the reports that I'd spent so much time compiling in the past were generated automatically. It was awesome. I had cut 360 work hours (15 clients × 2 hours × 12 months) over the next year. It was a huge project that took a ton of time, but the future time I saved was enormous.

For me, this was a great example of realigning priorities to accomplish something big. It would have been easy for me to just kick the can down the road and not implement a fix, but by focusing and realigning my priorities, I freed up an enormous amount of time. In the words of actor Scott Caan, "Good things happen when you get your priorities straight."

PROCRASTINATION IS A THIEF

Procrastination robs us of our time. We put things off because the big stuff looks hard, takes time, and is a lot of work.

I used to be terrible at procrastinating with schoolwork. I would tell myself that I worked better under pressure; therefore, I wasn't procrastinating. I believed I was doing my best work when I put it off to the last minute. What a bunch of crap! Most of the time something fun would come up, like baseball tickets or a party. While I was cramming at the last minute, I was still missing out on other fun.

I've met so many people who tell me they are procrastinators and will never be able to change. Anyone can change. They just aren't willing to give up something. You can always justify putting something off and finding reasons for why you should. But the sooner you realign your priorities, the sooner you'll be enjoying the fruits of having what you really want.

If you frequently get stuck in procrastination mode, try talking to others who've already completed the bigger project and can share systems or experiences that helped them in getting it done. A method I employ is to break down the project or task into smaller chunks.

My summer project this year is restoring a 1970 Honda CT-70 trail bike. It needs a lot of work. Instead of just jumping in and taking it apart, I'm making lists of what needs to be inspected and setting time aside to work on different parts of the bike. I'm breaking the entire project down into time slots that I can manage over the course of the summer. I'll be setting myself up for smaller victories (singles and doubles, remember?). I'll be consulting YouTube to learn from others the tips and tricks to make the job easier.

Learning from others' mistakes and advice can help you reduce the amount of time needed to complete your larger project. Lastly, try setting predetermined stopping points. These may be time based, such as the two-hour increments I used in my automated marketing report project.

When I started writing this book, I gave myself a goal of 2,000 words a week. I adjusted that goal to 3,000 words and have been diligently hitting my numbers each week.

SPONTANEITY IS FREEDOM

The last component of task prioritization is spontaneity. When I talk with people about the level of spontaneity in their lives, they tell me they wish they had more of it, but they just don't have the time. I always ask, "What's taking up your time?" They give me all sorts of excuses, but I know if I drilled down I could find hours of time in their lives if they just knew how to prioritize.

Spontaneity is very important, because it opens our minds to opportunities. Making time to be spontaneous means you have the ability to jump on opportunities when they present themselves.

For instance, because I built a new way for reporting to my clients, I've freed up thirty hours each month. That's a lot of time that I can now spend going to Cardinals games, riding my motorcycle, or taking Adriene out to dinner on a whim, just for fun.

By blocking out time on your calendar to get your work done, you will soon find that you have time to schedule open blocks. These open blocks can be used for work or enjoyment. I create an open block at 4:00 p.m. on Fridays to leave the office early and go enjoy something. It may be a glass of Scotch on my back deck or working on a fun project, but the point is I have the time planned to do whatever I want in the moment. Spontaneity is freedom, and it can only come from good planning and time management.

SEIZE THOSE OPPORTUNITIES

Every day is an opportunity to move closer to your goals. To seize that opportunity, take at least one action a day toward one of your goals. It also helps if you tell someone what you did. It reinforces your commitment.

When I'm training for Ironman, as long as I get to do a daily workout or stretching routine, I'm good. If you're reaching for a goal that is more abstract, such as making more money, be sure to take an action that will help you get there. The point is to take an action every day, no matter the size. Make it a priority.

YOUR LIFE IS YOUR OWN

WE'VE COME TO THE LAST CHAPTER OF THIS BOOK, BUT IT doesn't end here. Starting today, what are you going to do differently to make your life *yours* and start living it on your terms?

Motivational speaker Charlie Jones said, "You will be the same person in five years as you are today except for the people you meet and the books you read."

Shut Up and Go! has been your guide to finding out the who, the what, and, most of all, the how of realizing your dreams and living a fulfilling life. I hope it will continue to be. The lessons and exercises I've presented may take more than one reading, doing, and practicing to make them your own.

My goal has been to help you figure out what it is you really want, identify a plan for how to go out and get it, and develop the habits and follow-through to execute those wants.

If you stay focused and determined, you will reach your goals. I know from experience that focus requires turning down the temptations that take you off course. My temptations often come in the form of a fun night out with friends, buying stuff I don't need, or spending time with old friends who aren't geared the way I am and wind up draining my energy.

Determination requires following through when times get tough or your will is tested. My will is frequently tested in ways that seem insurmountable. I'm often presented with business challenges that I'm not sure our company will be able to overcome. Yet through it all, we persevere and thrive. We thrive because we have a set of core values that we hold true.

MAKING IT HAPPEN

If you want to be a better person, you have to learn how. If you want to make more money, you have to learn how. If you want to be happier, you have to learn how. Learning comes in two forms: reading and experience sharing.

Reading about new topics stimulates your brain and gives you ideas, and executing those ideas takes focus and determination. Meeting new people opens doors that sometimes you didn't even know could be opened. New people can share new perspectives you may not have been aware of.

When our company was going through a rough time maintaining a consistent cash flow, Derek and I met with one of our clients who is a wealth manager. He told us that we couldn't truly grow a service-based business without some form of compound recurring billing. We discussed several different options and settled upon a path of requiring a monthly retainer.

Within one year, we had enough clients on retainer to cover our overhead, salaries, and even 20 percent profit target. It was a painful year, but we stayed focused on building something that our clients valued on a recurring basis. And our client who shared that strategy with us is now a paying retainer client at the monthly figure he said we should strive for.

Reading and learning are great, but they are just a conduit for ideas. It's what you do with those ideas that matters. Remember our discussion in Chapter 1 about which comes first, thought or action? It's easy to think about making change, but there is no change without action.

Reading gives you thoughts, but it's the actions you take from those thoughts that actually change your life. Taking even just one small action a day puts you on a path toward accomplishing your goals.

If you want to get where you want to go even faster, you have to take bigger actions. In Chapter 11, I spoke of sacrifices. When I was coaching gymnastics and running SuiteCommute, I knew if I was ever going to have a chance of building my company, it would require my full attention. However, my only source of real income came from coaching.

It wasn't until I took the risk of quitting coaching and taking a personal loan that SuiteCommute started getting some traction. I was finally able to devote myself entirely to growing my start-up, and it worked. As it turned out, we grew to the point of attracting a buyer, and we eventually sold SuiteCommute.

You don't always have to make drastic changes like quitting your job, but the point is that drastic changes will get you to your goals faster.

When I was eighteen, I used to drink a twenty-ounce Mountain Dew every night before I went to bed. I knew it wasn't healthy, but I really liked it. One New Year's Eve, I decided I was going to give up drinking soda. For two weeks I experienced intense headaches and even developed a case of the shakes, but after those two weeks, I was fine. I have kept that commitment to not drinking soda (although I do have a little bit every now and then with an adult beverage), but I have not had a full can or bottle of soda since then. Come to think of it, I haven't had Mountain Dew since then.

GET OUT OF YOUR COMFORT ZONE

I believe that everyone has the potential to live life on their own terms, but unfortunately most people settle for less. People settle for bad relationships, crappy jobs, and stressful lives. They settle because they can't commit to making things better or they don't know how.

As I said in the introduction to this guide, *Shut Up and Go!* is all about the how. People don't become successes overnight. They must focus every day on achieving their dreams. By exploring your goals and aspirations, you create your own life path. Some people take only a few steps down that path. They find that the going is tough, so they turn and go back to their comfort zone.

Your comfort zone is where you like to operate. The car you drive, the clothes you wear, your level of health, and the money you make are all dictated by your comfort zone. You may want something different, but you're comfortable where you are. Don't be.

Many people I meet make just enough money to get by. They are often in major debt. When I ask them why, they list all sorts of reasons, but the truth is they're stuck. You can only get unstuck when you decide to step out of your comfort zone. Get uncomfortable. That's where growth in life comes from.

At twenty-seven, I started noticing some extra "love" in my love handles, and I realized I was growing considerably heavier. I decided I was uncomfortable at that weight and that I needed to find a way to lose it. I started eating less at dinner and signed up for a half Ironman. I began working out, and with my improved diet, I started losing weight. After my half Ironman, I fell back into my comfort zone and stopped working out. Four months later, I decided I needed a new goal to keep the weight off. So I signed up for a full Ironman. Setting that new goal was what I needed to get back in shape.

KEEP ON GOING

In Chapter 1, we talked about choice. You chose to read this book, to understand its principles, to do the exercises, and to learn the lessons I've shared. You chose to see it through to the end. You chose to say, "Shut up!" to all the voices and messages that say you can't. You chose not to accept limits. You chose to set goals and work toward them. You chose to go!

I truly believe you have the ability to be great. You can find success and, more importantly, self-fulfillment. When you align your life with your goals, you will get there. When you establish your core values and stick to them, you will make consistent progress every day toward the life you want. Your only limits are the ones you're willing to accept.

By acting instead of just dreaming, you can put into motion a force so powerful that nothing can stop you. That force is you. You can accomplish anything when you shut up and go!

ABOUT THE AUTHOR

BRANDON DEMPSEY is a serial entrepreneur and driving force behind the marketing firm goBRANDgo!, specializing in outsourced marketing services for privately held $10–100 million growth oriented companies. He is also the Chair of EO Accelerator, where he oversees a global program for entrepreneurship. Brandon's past startup companies include a remote work consulting company, a professional employers organization, a business continuity planning firm and a website development agency, all of which were either sold or merged into larger organizations.

Brandon is a featured thought leader in numerous online and print outlets, such as Forbes, Inc., and Huffington Post. When he isn't working, he spends his time training for Ironman triathlons and motorcycling around the world. Brandon lives in St. Louis with his wife Adriene and their three dogs.

Made in the USA
Middletown, DE
09 February 2019